13 Swing Trading Strategies

Pankaj Ladha

Anant Ladha

Published By

Invincible Publishers

Published by

Invincible Publication Pvt. Ltd.
201A, SAS Tower, Sector 38, Gurugram – 122003
Phone: +91-124-4034247, +91 9599066061
www.invinciblepublishers.com

Sales: Office No. 109 Prakash Mahal Ansari Road Daryaganj, Near ICICI Bank - 110002
Phone: +91-11-40198405
Email: invinciblepublishers@gmail.com

This book is a work of fiction. Names, characters, places and incidents are either the product of the author's imagination or are used fictitiously. Any resemblance to real persons, living or dead, or actual events or locations, is purely coincidental and the publisher does not hold responsibility for the same.

First edition –2022

ISBN: 978-93-90542-58-1

ACKNOWLEDGEMENT

The book "13 Swing trading strategies" has been special project for me, since last 5 years I was considering to write a book on stock market. The person who motivated me and told me to go ahead was none other than My lovely son Anant Ladha. He not only motivated me but also put in many hours of hard work to produce the book. Dear Anant, Your focus & commitment to goal made it happen.

To Hemchand ji Jain who has been my second teacher of stock market. After Papa I deeply value your good work, vision and image of right thinking person.

To Nimesh Shah who is CEO of ICICI AMC and has been our biggest well wisher and supporter. I have learnt basics of market and investor behavior from him.

To Shankar Naren CIO of ICICI AMC, who has always helped in understanding fundamentals and concept of contrarian investing in much better way.

To Aashish P. Sommaiyaa, CEO WhiteOak who is like a brother, friend and guide.

To Nilesh Shah, CEO Kotak AMC who always helps in understanding the market since 1992 from era of Harshad Mehta and is always there to guide and support.

To Kalpen Parekh, CEO DSP AMC who is always appreciating to our ideas and helps in better understanding of investors behavior.

To Sunil Subhramaniam, CEO Sundaram AMC who has helped in deepening the knowledge about market cycles and always a big well wisher for us.

To Pritam Kumar Goswami, my childhood friend and author of "Sunrise with in you" and "Millionaire Mind Unleashed". For always telling me to write my experience in the form of book.

To our clients whom we consider as family members, for showing faith on me. "your faith always inspires me."

And of course

To my team members for believing in Invest Aaj For Kal and giving your services to the organization. I deeply value your support and serving the clients making Invest Aaj For Kal a National and international brand.

Pankaj Ladha

I would like to send my heartfelt and the most special, sincere thanks to all the Subscribers and Viewers of Invest Aaj For Kal, you all are my extended family now and your motivation is something which allows me to think beyond limits and generate creative ideas. You are my real source of motivation to spread financial literacy in the world.

Thank you for your endless faith and love!!

Extended gratitude to friends Raj Shamani, Pranjal Kamra, Rachna Ranade, Vivek Bajaj, Pushkar Thakur & Rishab Jain who have been amazingly supportive and pillar of strength for me through my journey of social media.

To my father in law, Late Swayam Rathi who will always be my biggest motivator and support. He is always my motivation to work harder and hussle in life.

Last but not the least, I would also like to say special thanks to Invincible Publication Pvt. Ltd from the bottom of my heart and soul. It was just an idea until it got printed and published.

Anant Ladha

Contents

SWING TRADING

PART-1

CHAPTER 1

SWING TRADE- THE BEGINNER PERSPECTIVE

In simple language, a swing trade is like taking advantage of a temporary situation in stocks price action. Sometime people confuse it with position trading but actually it's for quite lesser duration than that. As we all know that intra-day trade lasts for a single day and Position trading last for around 3 to 10 weeks which tries to give profits due to a medium-term price action in a stock, swing trade lies somewhere between both of these say around 1 to 3 weeks.

The way it works

Generally speaking, a swing trader would like to get more juice out of a stock than a day trader and would be satisfied with lesser than a long-term position trader. Swing trader would make their money from market generated anomalies in the medium or long-term trend. For example, if a stock is in an intact bull run of medium or long term and certain technical or fundamental events happen in market which drags the broader market lower. Considering the situation very temporary this event will give the swing trader an opportunity to short the stock and vice versa. These kinds of events are generally like Budget, IIP data etc. which does not hold a long-term impact on the stock and gives a small and temporary downtick or uptick to the trader. Important point to be noted is that swing trade trends does not impact long and medium-term charts of a stock.

Swing traders & Day traders

The notable difference between a swing trader and a day trader is about volume of the moves and position sizing. A day trader works on very small gain either via shorting or buying, these gains can even be as low as 1% to 3% in the stock. To maintain substantial gains in these kind of price movements a day trader has to take large positions in the stock. Simply, to make profit of Rs. 10,000 on movement of Rs 1 on a stock a trader will have to trade in 10,000 quantities. On the other hand, a swing trader works on better margin and larger than intra-day move on a stock, so he has luxury to trade even smaller volumes.

Another notable difference is that a day trader would not consider holding a stock overnight as a nightmare and he is essentially working on intra-day movement and his chart reading is also restricted to that. He would cut the position even in losses but shall not carry it for next day. Contrary to that a swing trader would buy the stock to be held for around seven days.

Swing Trader & Position Trader

In comparison to a swing trader, a position trader will hold stock for a longer period of time. He will not get worried by small movements in price of a stock, even if the movement is upto 10%. He has bought the stock for medium or long term and wants to capture a big price gain. On the contrary a swing trader is essentially looking for gains in the range of 8 to 12% and not looking to hold the stock for more than 1 to 3 weeks even if he sees strong price and volume action. They also believe that they must cut the losses very fast in case their reading has gone wrong and the stock movement has reversed.

A swing trading system may work with a risk/reward ratio of around 1:3. In contrast, a position trader might prefer 1:3 on the low side and look for 1:5 risk/reward ratio that work with lower winning percentages. For example, a swing trader will look in profits when a chart gets overbought at Relative Strengths reading.

Basically, as swing trader has taken position in a stock because he has read some small contra short term movements in a stock, very less likely is that he would go further and convert the position into to position trading.

A position trader will have quite larger time and price horizon than swing traders, these traders essentially work on capturing a long-term fundamental story of a stock. A swing trader will derive his position from charts which will tell him about a short term move where a position trader will analyse Sales and EPS growth type of factors which will decide medium to long term trajectory of the companies' performance.

When to trade swings?

Swing trading is essentially for those traders who can't wait for a longer term to make gains out of stock or those who can't be so accurate to predict or read charts for very fast-moving intra-day markets. As discussed, earlier swing traders will hold a stock in general for not more than a week or three and their stop losses are also decided in the same fashion. They keep their ratio of loss to profit to around 1:3. Say if as a swing trader I am looking for an 8 to 12% gain in a swing trade I will be ready to keep 3% to 4% as a stoploss. A swing trader would like to cut their losses and sit on cash if the market moves contrarian to their stock call.

Even in very much roaring bull markets a swing trader would not like to convert his position into a position trade. The purpose of his trade is to enter and exit with in one to three weeks before trend reverses.

Choice on becoming "A type of trader"

Making choices while entering into markets is always a tough call as markets gives variety of opportunities to every market participant. Investing is a different domain but while trading you need to choose trading strategy very cautiously. Discussing about intra-day trading I must say that it's a very tough job and you need to be on toes for it. It needs a lot of screen time or rather I must say that you cannot have luxury to stay away from the screen for more than 10-15 minutes, you left the screen and you might lose the opportunity. Besides this you must have an expertise in reading intra-day charts as it requires in-depth analysis as you are looking for almost hidden trades.

On the other hand, other type of trades is for a bit medium term and one might not have patience to hold the trade. In this situation swing trade works as a balancing act. A trader has to read less charts and probability of finding an opportunity is quite high. Reading daily charts is far easier than reading an hourly chart. In swing trade money can be made with less efforts.

Chapter 2

Why to choose swing trading?

Swing trading can be a good fit for people of all experience levels because it has many benefits over other trading methods. There are basically three major aspect of a trading method- Risk Management, Psychology and System Management. The toughest to manage is psychological aspect of trade. It allows you to stay calm in most of the situations. The trader therefore always has to select a trade where he knows his Stoploss, Profits to be expected and duration which are of comfort for him. The most important peace factor for a trader in swing trade is that you need not to be glued to the screen and get time to square off trade before it's too late.

A day trader Vs. Swing Trader

Just imagine you woke up on a day, had some breakfast got a good workout and yoga session, Market opened, You watched it for few minutes and did not see any position to be squared off which you bought as a swing trade. You switch on the TV and relax for the entire day. This is what you can do if you are a swing trader. The only thing which you will have to do is to set an alarm of certain technical chart levels on any mobile trading app you use, which will allow you to know when the time to square off the position is.

On the other hand, day trading is like going to office from 9 to 5 or even more than that, that too without taking any break. As we discussed earlier that day traders works on very range bound movements of a stock price, they can't afford to get their eyes off the screen. A day trader must be so alert that even one percent move on stock price can either make or break the trading day. It has got the thrill factor but at the same time it is way too risky and engagement-based activity. Also, if you are involved in any other business or have a full-time job, day trading is surely not for you. You might feel that day trading means squaring of your trades in a day, I will say day trading is where you have to give your complete day to trading.

The risk in swing trading as compared to other trading style

Swing traders do not have to take very large position like day traders as they have good number of days to make money out of a stock price movement. If a swing trader is expecting 8 to 12% gain from a stock, he can spread it over 7 to 21 days which barely means 1% or even less per day movement in stock prices. On the other hand, while being in a bear market which we keep experiencing every now and then, the swing trader does not have to keep holding the share for long as swing trader's time horizon is far shorter than position trader and very long-term investors. He does not have to keep notional losses on his holding. If the exit triggers are there, the position is to be squared off.

Risk capital is another aspect of swing trade, when we compare it to day trade, we see that the amount of money at stake is far less as we have already discussed that day trader works on very thin profit margin and a swing traders expect around 8 to 12% of price movement in the stock. So, the amount of capital at risk is always less. On the other hand, a position trader is always stuck in notional losses. A position trader's strategy does not allow him to sell stock in losses very soon but a swing trader can always do that and convert positions on cash, generally swing traders are always cash rich as they keep looking for buying opportunity. It's like having hot money which keeps chasing best available profit opportunity in the market and not committed to any sector or economic growth story.

For example,

With a 10 day moving average over 20 day moving average crossover signal, as swing trader would lock in profits around the 70 Relative Strengths (RS). In contrast, a position trader would stay in the trend until the 10-day EMA crossed back under the 20-day EMA.

Another important difference between a position trader and swing trader is that a positional trader is like a sugar cane juice seller who won't throw the sugar cane until every drop of juice is extracted out of it. A position trader will hold the share until it reaches peak of that trend and there are no major trend reversal signs. On the other hand, a swing trader is looking for first lot of fresh juice and sells it for a higher price so that he gains in overall scenario. So, a swing trader is looking for cream of the milk and looking for those momentums in the stock which gives him a chance to earn profits in range of 8 to 12%.

If we compare the overall performance report of the swing trader vs. position trader, we may find that on total a swing trader will end up earning more as he is ready to encash the opportunities and looking for hot short-term gains. A position trader will look for overall gains in a longer term which on an average will not be that much of gains which a swing trader may earn given by cumulative profits of swing trades.

In simple words we can say that a swing trader will always look forward to book profits and a position trader will be looking at his profits fluctuating with the market moves, going up and down. Position traders will be working on notional profit and loss and at the end when positions are squared off, he might end up making average profits which may be lower than total of swing traders.

Keep looking at your risk!

As we have already discussed that swing trader shall be holding the shares overnight unlike the day traders. In general, the charts tell that a stock's movement can be tracked or predicted better when the matter is of overnight holding. It's always very difficult to predict charts points for day trading and that is what makes day trading very risky. This asks the trader to engage more of risk capital.

Situational choice of trading method

A trader has to do one thing only which is to trade. By any strategy he has to get into the market and pick few stocks to trade for the day or few upcoming days. But one very important aspect is about choosing what kind of trading strategy the trader is going to adopt. It is simple yet a process-based activity for a trader. It involves some scientific methods. First of all, the trader must make a watch list and observe the price and volume activity of the list. At different times same stock might behave completely different from its last pattern of price and volume movement.

Once the trader is conversant with this than time horizon works as a very important tool for trading method selection. Most of the day traders spend full day to screen trading. On the other hand a swing trader will not be spending a lot of time to choose a trade rather he will prefer to get alarmed about certain levels of price and volume movement and then enter or exit in the stock.

Timing is always very important for day trader specifically because as we discussed earlier the day traders works on very thin margins and might miss money making opportunities if they are not prompt on market. On the other hand, it's equally important tool for swing trader also as your profit or loss depends a lot on which stage of the swing did you enter the stock in. If it is the last lag of the swing then the overall trade becomes use less for a swing trader because in any case, he would not be happy for 2-3% gains and very thin stop losses.

Earning Per Hour

In business, time is money and in stock markets if you are not valuing your time then either you will never make money or will end up earning peanuts. A day trader as we have been discussing needs a lot of time to monitor the price actions. Even though they work on very large amount of monetary and share volumes they always work on very thin margins. There are many instances of day trading on daily basis in the market where 1 lac shares are bought and sold within the gap of half rupee and the trader finally made Rs. 50,000 for the day. Because of this a day trader needs a lot of screen time, just like a gatekeeper who has to be on duty always or their might be a security threat. If we take around 6.5 hours of trading in markets for everyday a day trader has margin of taking around one hour break only, that too when he is not holding any position which make his earning per hour very low and make him a lesser productive trader. On the other hand, a swing trader does not have to spend more than 1 hour on daily basis which ends up his earning per hour on a very higher level.

Looking for the timing

Swing trading is quite beneficial and profitable than other methods of trading as it has a lot of advantages, some of the advantages are mentioned as following:

1. It keeps your brain at work for lesser time due to lesser requirement of screen time. We must agree that even if someone enjoys trading in stock, a break is always a much-needed thing. On the other hand, the risk capital is also very low because of higher percentage of expected gains.

2. In swing trading, entry and exit signals can be executed at the open or close and requires small increments of time. These points make it a great starting point for aspiring traders with jobs.

3. A swing trader at times can get into day trading activity always, depending on his current status of activity in swing trade positions taken by him.

4. Swing traders have the freedom to execute signals anywhere on the basis of their strategy parameters. They could do so at the close, open or in combinations of both.

5. Capital consideration is always lower than other forms of trade and time management is quite easier as you don't have to be on toes always to track the price movement of a share.

The IQ , EQ and your body

Why we prefer swing trading always over day trading and position trading is because day trading is physically difficult path and medium-term growth investing is emotionally difficult path while long term value investing like Buffet is intellectually difficult path.

Why investing like ace investor Warren Buffet is very difficult is that, it is very difficult to think and act like him. It needs a lot and lot of patience to work in their style and overall, everyone does not have that intellect. In a recent example when Zee entertainment and Tata Motors crashed in 2020-21, Indian investor Rakesh Jhunjhunwala enhanced his stake in companies and the result is all in front of us. The stocks zoomed since then. An eagle's eye on company's cash flow, market scenario and economic environment study is so deeply rooted in their thinking is that they know what indicators to see and how to study those. Also the amount of time they spend in studying about a single stock is genuinely not possible for all of us.

Here, Emotional Intelligence which is taught in business schools with so much emphasis works a lot, you need to control your emotions about the market and stocks. Sometime when most of the crowd is behaving in singular manner, we need to take a contra call. For instance, during COVID times those who had emotionally stable thinking and analyzed the market well are at least millionaire. Everyone was selling, Specially FIIs as they had their own global issues and the pace of COVID was quite faster in their domestic markets but few investors and mutual funds kept buying and we all can see the results. So, always work with I.Q and keep your E.Q under control.

Learn to go against the most common theory in the market, because historical evidence says that bear market starts when the market is in most euphoric conditions ever. Don't go after FOMO (Fear of Missing Out), Keep your I.Q. tracking the stock and you will always get a chance. This is why swing trading is very beneficial, it always gives you a chance to trade well in both bullish and bearish zone.

Always remember that long term investing is very difficult because most of the investors cannot control their E.Q. Sometime they will buy a stock and won't sell it until it crashes 90% or sometime, they don't have patience to keep holding a stock until it becomes a multi bagger. People kept on buying Vodafone even when the telecom market was in the woods and they could not hold Deepak nitrite when it was on the way to become multi bagger. Remember, Market is always overbought or oversold in some of the time zone, it is the trader who need to identify the opportunities with a cool head and buy at the right times for right time horizon.

Another type of trading which follows physically difficult path is day trading. This form of trading is also very tough as it needs lot of engagement. To understand this, we need to simulate the overall day schedule of a day trader who has to be on the toes and always have to keep reading the screen. As the market open at 9 AM, he has to sit in front of the screen compulsorily till 3:30 PM until the last trade happens that too without a break because in an uncertain environment you do not know which news wants you to sell or buy, the Indian market does not close and meanwhile European wakes up and then gradually American market and SGX Nifty starts trading which is a job to be tracked at least till 12 midnight or 1 AM and very next day early morning Dow closing and Dow Futures and SGX nifty are to be tracked again. This goes on and on.

Now think, did you enter into markets to do this? Then why not any 9 to 5 job? Which will at least give you some time and week off to see the life beyond computer screen. A day trader is always active even at the closing of market, because practically the entire world markets are connected to each other and movement in one market impacts the other one. This twenty-four hour job makes day trading a tough affair to deal with.

So chose your trading type wisely between all three!

Chapter 3

The Stoploss- Don't travel beyond this

This is the first and foremost rule to be followed while trading in stocks, cutting losses on a level is as important as breathing for living. By doing this you will be able to protect your capital and be able to trade further and can live another day as a trader. Stop loss is like your insurance.

If you are not ready to take stop loss just stop here either prepare yourself for stop loss as mentioned in the book religiously. Otherwise, do not read the book further.

Following the concept of the stoploss is far more important than trading itself. Not following the stoploss is like collecting stale grains in your godown expecting that someday it will come back in good condition and you will profit it out.

1. **Feel good about the Stoploss if triggered** - This is the most important issue while we discuss about the stoploss, no one wants to lose, and rather I must say that no one feels good while losing and this is what puts us into deeper losses. In various bear markets a lot of traders kept on holding the positions and did not want to exit the position in losses keeping a false hope that someday the market will recover and their trades will get back into green or at least those will recover to price they paid. If you have same feeling then you are also suffering from price paid bias.

This false hope keeps the trader busy looking at the stock price just hoping. It is just hoping not investing and we are in the business of investing and not hoping. Hoping against the hope. Larger issue is that people get emotional while trading and get connected to a particular stock or story and don't want to take a losing trade. For example, DHFL was a stock which made huge money for investors with gaining around 1000% from between 2013 and 2018, the fall started in 2018 and those who did not work on the stoploss lost everything what they earned even something out of pocket also. Believe me 80% of your trades are also very good, but just 20% of the trades where you don't put stop losses eats up your complete profits.

Yes bank, we all remember was a great company at one time, the stock gained almost 700% between 2013 and 2018 and lost 95% of value between 2018 to 2021. PC Jewellers, Cox and kings, Sintex, Vakrangee, Eros international are no different stories, after being multi bagger these stocks lost almost entire gains but only for those who did not follow the stoploss in their trade. Rest all got saved.

Another wonderful example of importance of the stoploss comes from recent IPOs in 2021-22, like PayTm, Zomato, Latent view, Fino payment bank, Sarvodaya small finance bank, Car trade, Policy Baazar. The market was so exuberant when Zomato got listed and the stock almost doubled on listing day itself, Nykka followed the path and Policy Bazaar showed decent gains. When PayTm hit the market the situation changed and the spill over effect came on almost all the new age tech companies. If stop loss was taken care of at that time some investor would not have lost 2/3 of their invested amount in PayTm.

This is a long-term or positional trade example and on the similar lines you will find a lot of swing trading example where traders don't want to book losses because they don't like keeping the stop losses in place.

Why people do not use the stoploss? What I learnt from my experience, When you invest money in any stock you just do not invest money you also invest your emotions, your ego and your pride and all these will tell you there is nothing wrong in your stock, you will think that it is taking support at 50 DMA or 200 DMA or you will think that you are buying business not stock and so on. Company is doing well there is no reason why my stock will not come back, I am long term investor or I am still getting my dividend. With this type of thinking I feel you are just asking for trouble.

As the greatest investor of his time Jesse Livermore said "You hope when you should fear and you fear when you should hope" To explain this when your stock is up you should be hoping that you made right decision and it will go higher in spite of fearing that my profit may wipe out. And when your stock is down you should be fearing that it may go down further instead of hoping that it might bounce back.

The market does not care what you think or what you hope, market will do what it wants to do. You cannot direct the market, you are just a small fish in the sea. So, to survive you need to follow the time-tested rules with edge to survive. We must know that market is not going to die, we all are temporary and market is not. If you book losses today then in future the market will give you thousands of more opportunities to earn. Remember if you book loss, you are not a bad trader. But if you keep your ego and emotion at the forefront than your capital will vanish someday and you will not be able to take another trade.

2. **Selling the winners and holding onto the losers** - Suppose you have to invest in two different individuals, one of those is a common graduate and the other one come's from the pedigree of IIT. The IITian got a job of Rs. 25K per month and the graduate also somehow got a job of Rs. 25K per month because his father was in a private company and owner of that company give appointment on the basis of his father's reputation. One year after that The IITian got a 100% pay hike and reached at 50K per month, at the same time, the graduate also got a pay hike of 20% and reached at 30K per month. Where will you invest now?

   A lot of traders" mentality will be that The IITian has got a good pay hike and money has been doubled and they feel it is time to book profit, hence money will get withdrawn. And hold where the salary is just 30k in expectation of it will also touch 50k soon. But the fact is IITian will get faster increments even in future. This is a very common mistake which people do. They sell their best performing stock first and keep betting on less performing.

   This is what is so true about the trade also, some trade which are either taken at the wrong point or by the time got into red zone, a trader must not keep holding it. Sell it and relax. Just because it's your trade does not mean that it will always perform. You must be so ready to close a trade which is not making money, don't sacrifice your mental peace just for a trade. Remember, your life is far more important than these things. If you will cut the loss, you will be relaxed and ready to take lot of fresh trades which will probably make money for you.

3. **Social media and news sites are not the place to trade-** Another thing which forces a trader is social media and a lot of news circulating around. Suppose you took a trade and it starts making losses, meanwhile you heard somewhere that this particular trade is going to make money in coming days. Till now you were a disciplined trader and was ready to exit the stock because it triggered your stoploss target, but now...

   You are not selling it because someone said that it will make money, you keep holding a trade and someday the same news item comes up with a sorry and asks you to cut the position. Before this you were having your own style of trade and your own conviction about it, by getting influenced you just lost more. Have your own convictions about the trade and don't get swayed by someone. Probably you will have more money in your pocket. No one will care about your money more then you. Having conviction on your own conviction is the key. Nothing big was ever achieved without it.

4. **You need to pay fee to learn-** Getting a degree is never free, at least if you want quality education. This stands so true for stock markets also. Remember, there are no free lunches in the world. Though you don't pay anything directly here but the losses which you make while following the stoploss can be considered a learning remuneration for the market, so never think that your losses went wasted,

it brought you an insight and knowledge which you will use to make more money. Remember the best teacher in stock market is your last loss-making trade. So, think it like, in stock market either you earn or you learn. Which will make you better trader in future.

5. **It takes time to become a Pro-** Sachin did not become Sachin in a single day, even after becoming the best in world he has to face too many failures. The best batsman of the world did not go well as a captain and finally had to give it up. Same thing holds true for a stock trader also. Give yourself time, the markets will teach you provided you have patience to learn from your mistakes. Don't get obsessed what happened in past either good or bad, the rear-view mirror is only for a status check, at the end you have to drive forward only. According to my experience a day trader needs 10,000 hours screen experience, while a swing trader need 2,000 hours of chart reading experience to become a successful trader. Give time its time and everything will slowly start falling in place.

As a trader you must always remember that markets are not concerned whether you have been trading for last 50 years or 50 days, it will behave the way it has to. It is not concerned to save your hard-earned money, only you can save it by cutting your losses on time. Don't fall in an ego trap, it does not allow you to be wrong and being wrong in market is not a bad thing, it is like falling diving while taking a catch. You will get bruised but the elation of taking a catch will let you forget all the pains.

I meet a lot of young traders who will say that they feel very bad when they sell any stock in loss and the feeling is worse when just after they sell and the stock takes a U-turn, I tell them what if the stock would not have taken a U-turn and shelved your 50% of capital? Yes, let's accept that its part of the game. It's just like buying life Insurance, you won't die to get money from the insurer, would you? Same way you take a fire insurance policy because you don't want to see yourself not being able rebuilt if it is burnt. When we suggest to cut loss making positions below 3 to 4% below your buying price in swing trades, we feel like you spent that amount on insuring your capital.

Another very important point which is very basic mathematics and still people ignore to understand the same is about a stock's fall and rise percentage, I agree that a lot of stocks rebound good after falling good, how much good is good for your losses to be recovered. Let's understand this with following table

Stock's Fall %age	Stock's gain %age required to reach on same level
10	11.11
20	25
25	33
50	100
75	300
80	400

I hope, I don't have to say much after this, just imagine you did not honour your stoploss and the stock fell upto 50%, to reach on the same level it needs to ride by 100%, if something fell by 75% than it will have to become triple to come back on the same price. How many stocks you have ever had in your portfolio which have tripled?

What can you do to save yourself from devasting losses that will happen to almost all investors? I do not know about you but I know only one method and that is to have a proper 3 to 1 profit and loss ratio. By doing so if you are right only 33% in your trades you will stay in the game.

Jim Simons is renowned to be the best trader of modern era. No one even Warren Buffett, Peter Lynch, Ray Dalio, Steve Cohen, or George Soros could match his performance. Since 1988, his Renaissance's signature Medallion fund has generated average annual returns of 66 percent, which is unmatched.

The fund is so good in its performance that it charges heavy annual fee and after that fee investors got net 39% return on investment. This is amazing, significantly better than Warren Buffet.

So the question arises is that is Jim Simons better than Warren Buffett? If we compare the average holding period of both of them than Jim Simons is far more successful than Warren Buffet. It is very important to discuss that the average holding period for Jim Simons is just two days. That is why I feel swing trading can be more profitable than buy and hold investors.

Another thing which Jim Simons proves that you don't have to be right more than 90% time to be right. You will be surprised to know that Jim Simons success ratio was around 51% only.

6. **To cut a long story short:** - Don't worry, if you are losing 3 to 4% in swing trading, markets are filled with wealth creation capacities, covering your 3 to 4% is not a big deal for it. Always remember that the rule of the stoploss is always same even if you are buying the best performing stock or the best name of market.

Every day in market is a new day, when you purchased a banking stock last week in a normal scenario you never thought that in upcoming week inflation number will be high and RBI will surprise you with a sudden rate hike, situation changes and so our stand should also change. So, sell whenever it is required to, it's only about selling a stock in loss that too when it is necessary. So don't feel bad about it. Don't take it personally, do not take your bad trade to your bed. Just exit and sleep well.

Do not get confused, this book is being written for swing trader so we look for a target of 8-12% and stoploss at 3-4%. If you are positional investor or trader you may take target 20-30% and stop loss as 8-10%. Even in bad market condition for swing trade you may keep target 7-8% and stop loss at 2-3%.

Chapter 4

How much to lose to earn a rupee

Measuring risk and reward while trading is utmost important activity, a trader always must know what he will lose if the trade goes against him and what he is going to make if the market conditions are favorable to his trade. Technically risk reward ratio is an assessment of how much money you have to keep on table to get into a trade which will give you desired profit. So this gives you a worst and best case scenario. Let's understand the system with the help of an example.

If a trade is taken on 100 shares of a Rs.1,000 stock and the stoploss is set at the Rs.970 and the price target for the stock is Rs 1,090, then the risk is Rs.3,000 if the trade triggers the stoploss as the trader will lose Rs. 30 per share. On the other hand the reward could be Rs.9,000 if the price target is reached as the trader will take home Rs. 90 per share.

In general, a trader can keep a risk reward ratio of 1:3. So, in %age terms the stoploss to be kept in the range of around 3-4% on least and gain target to be at around 8 to 12% of traded amount.

The risk reward for a swing trader can be termed in monetary terms but it can have another form which is time. For example, a trader can hold a profit-making winning trade from 3 to 9 or 7 days to 21 days and a losing trade from 1 to 3 or 1 to 7 days. This terms your risk and reward ratio for time also. In the above example it comes out to be 1:3 as it came in terms of monetary gains and loss.

Ascertainment of a risk reward ratio is one of the key parameters of success for a trader. It is not an exercise which is only a number game rather it's the premise on which a swing traders' overall efficiency will depend. The objective of doing it is to maximise profitable trades and minimise losing trades of a swing trader. More of profitable trades will keep good monetary reserves for a trader in bad times. The best part about risk-reward ratio is that it gives you a stoploss which keeps losses small and keep traders disciplined.

Always keep your risk reward ratio in tight limits as it will give you chances to be into monetary positions and be ready to take advantage of right movement in the stock to be bought.

There are three different ways of quantifying a risk-reward ratio. Which are following:

1. Managing a trade
2. Back Testing
3. Measuring past trading results is one edge that a trader can have to create a good reward at entry and manage it as the trade plays out.

With this there are certain outcomes also:

1. A very minimum loss in case the trader's stoploss is triggered as the range of the stoploss is around 3-4% only.

2. A small win if the trade moves in their favour before reversing and triggering a trailing stop.

3. A huge profit in case the stock hits the decided profit target or you trail and it keep going up in favour of your trade.

While trading in the markets some of the investor works with their E.Q. "Emotional Quotient" whereas they must work with their I.Q. "Intelligence Quotient". This I.Q. can be coined as determination of Risk-Reward ratio. Most of the investor lose money even in good stocks and even in good market waves because they don't follow the discipline of Risk-Reward ratio or the stoploss and profit target strategy.

If you go into the market with this, you will never lose big because you have the stop losses in place which will minimise your loss. Another important part is that as a trade reaches a profit target, the remaining reward may now be less than the potential risk if the chart becomes overbought which signals that the stock must be sold and profits to be booked.

This strategy always allows us to keep a check that we need to take minimum risk to earn maximum profits. The least amount of risk capital is at stake and chances of profits are highest.

The back testing- Journey to the past

We always keep listening in the stock market that whatever has worked in past may not work in future, simply meaning that the amount of returns which any stock or broader markets have produced in past may not be repeated in future. So, the point comes is that while trading we should always look forward. According to my experience History always repeat in the market. Reason is very simple, Human nature and emotions never change. Whenever your own money is on the bet, it is normal to be emotional. But the market does not know who you are, and it does not care what you think or what you would like to see happening in the market.

Let me again remind you what Jesse Livermore said "There are only two emotions in the market – hope and fear. The problem is you hope when you should fear, and you fear when you should hope. This is a costly mistake. When your stock fall 4% from your cost when you swing trade and you are losing money you hope it will come back at least to your buy price. While your stoploss mechanism telling you that it is time to be fearful, that you might lose more money, just exit. On the other side when a stock goes up in your favour and you are making money you book profit on fear that you might lose money which you earned in books. It is time you must be thinking that you actually found real winner which can give you big money. It is time to hope.

Question appears that how to overcome such costly emotions. That is why reading history is important and you should be establishing buying and selling rules derived from historical research – In this book we will discuss many time-tested swing trading strategies. Doctors, lawyers study the history and use that for future success. Stock market is no different from it. You should use it in your swing trade. Reading history will not only give you best of the profits but also will teach how not to have large losses. While reading history in trading history we may call it back testing which is a kind of simulation of your pre-decided Risk-Reward scenario. In back testing we apply our trading strategy and risk-reward strategy to a stock on its past performance and historical charts. With this a trader shall test whether the decided strategy is strategy with edge to generate profit or not or at least it will save the trader from big losses.

Whenever your money is on the bet it is natural to be emotional and your ego is also invested with your money, the stock market is no exception. So ignore what you think or what is the personal opinion of supposed expert, tips or insider report. You know the strategies which worked well in past and that may probably be effective in future if you are ready to accept that you or your strategy is not going to be right every time and when it seems to be wrong you trigger your stoploss and just exit.

A swing trader should conduct back testing on good amount of data which may start from one month to 5 year or in certain cases it may go up to 10 or 20 years of data. A trader must check its strategy on various charts level as well as on different market scenario like Bull market, Bear market, Volatile markets, Inflationary scenarios and many more.

Finally-It's all about numbers

Another important method of keeping a check on your Risk-Reward ratio is to keep a track on the final outcome of your trading, which can be termed as quantifying the result of trading. It is like opposite of back testing where you test the outcome unlike checking on the already available data. A minimum of 20 to 30 trades taken by the trader can be a good sample size. It's very simple to do so, a trader has to combine the data of winning trade and losing trades along with the amount of money made and lost on average in each trade.

If your average losing trade was 3% of the price from entry and your average winning trade was 6% of the price at entry, then you have a 1:2 risk/reward ratio in your trading results, which would be a great place to start.

Following trading example can be considered for a study:

Winning Trades:

+10%

+5%

+6%

+4%

Equals +25% in gains on capital at risk.

Losing Trades:

-5%

-2.5%

-3%

-2%

Equals -12.5% in losses on capital at risk.

Losing-12.5% versus making 25% equals a 1:2 risk/ratio by the percentage of capital in previous trades.

A swing trader with a 1:2 risk to reward ratio only needs a 33%-win rate to break even and can be profitable with a 50%-win rate.

For example:

Make +Rs.2000

Lose-Rs.1000

Lose –Rs.2000

Make +Rs.4000

Lose –Rs.1000

Lose –Rs.2000

Equals Rs.0 break even with a 1:2 risk/reward ratio and 33%-win rate.

Another example:

Make +Rs.2000

Lose –Rs.1000

Make + Rs.2000

Make +Rs.4000

Lose - Rs.1000

Lose - Rs.2000

Equals Rs.4000 profit with a I:2 risk/reward ratio and 5o %-Win rate.

Such type of simple risk reward ratio will offset losses with the gain and it will provide all defence you need. By doing so you will be gaining more real market working experience than if you just buy one stock and hold it for very very long term. I started my career in 1989 since then a lot of fancy and so called blue chip companies have vanished from market. Yes bank, Unitech, PC Jewellers, Vakrangee all these are recent examples from well-known blue-chip list and gave great return to shareholders. All were traded above 400 during peak now changing hands below 40. So much of pain for buy and hold investors.

Most important thing to focus on

No one likes to be wrong or accept that he was wrong on buying at first place. Always do post analysis of your trades every month and every year so that you can learn from your winner as well as losers. If you do not look at what mistake you have done you will never become a better trader. While analysing the trading journal and his strategy a trader must keep a record of both loosing and winning trades. Try to find out what you have done right on the trades that went up and what you were doing wrong where you lost.

A good trader has three qualities:

1. Having a good risk/reward ratio like 1:3.
2. He is managed to allow the trade to play out as planned. If you have a trading plan but you do not follow it is equalling to having no plan.
3. He follows a time-tested strategy which have edge in the market.

Why has "Cut your losses short and let your winners run" been such a popular saying with traders since the time of Jesse Livermore? Simply because it tells you about a great risk reward strategy which will make money for you. Still, we all are humans and may not take the best path to reach to our destination always.

A lot of trader consider that following a good strategy is very tough job, they have to be so intelligent like Dr. APJ Abdul Kalam to find a good strategy. In fact it is so simple to decide on a good trading strategy, what is more important is to stick to it and not deviating from the path.

Important thing is to keep simple 3:1 profit loss target. It is the most difficult lesson for investors to learn and what I experienced in my 30 years of career that 80% investor cannot let go their ego and never learn this important lesson. This becomes the genesis of loss making, and that is why most of them have 80% of looser in portfolio and never produce good results in direct stock investing or trading.

SWING TRADING

PART-2

Identifying of trades

Be good about timing,

Make your every trade a best one & earn out of it

TOP 13 TRADING STRATEGIES – INDEX

INTRODUCTION

Different Trading Strategies-

Stock markets are not same every day, every month or even in a year. The markets will always behave in a different manner at times due to the factors working behind it. With this, we also need to change our approach and strategy to deal with the markets. We must do it because we want best result all the times. If we keep on adopting the same strategy in all type of markets then at the end we might either make sub normal profits or even loses. As the old saying is "Be a Roman when you are in Rome".

If the market is not same than how it will be possible to do the same thing daily in the market? With changing market, we need to change our strategies, we need to change the way we think or rather the way we execute. From the great recession to the global meltdown in 2008 to 2020 COVID flash crash, the market has faced several bruises and several moments of elation that has constantly changed its nature and as a trader we are bound to change the way we deal with the market because we are nothing but just a tiny part of the market.

This is an important part of the learning for all of the traders and every trader must keep learning to be sustainable in the market. The biggest mistake which new traders does is to expect everything too quickly, another problem is that most of the new traders enter the market while the market is in Bull Phase and for next few months everyone earns until market takes a breather.

Under such circumstances, a trader is likely to commit the following five money losing mistake:

- Trade larger than the risk capacity, one must bite that much only that he can chew.
- Trading like playing blind in the market, actually trading without any strategy.
- Unlimited trading, getting addicted to it.
- Loving penny stocks with an expectation that it will become a multi-bagger.
- Borrow and trade without understanding the risk of capital eradication.

Discipline works?

It is generally considered that being discipline and having risk management always works well in market, but this is only one aspect of success in stock markets. A good trading strategy must be mixed with these factors to earn better. A trader must always remember that discipline mixed with bad trading strategy is always a losing proposition. If a trader learns about how to adopt different strategies in different market conditions then around 90% of the job is done. Firstly, we must learn to recognise the market trend and then immediately adopt a strategy which suits it.

If you see the market very closely than it has four behavioural pattern– Bullish, Neutral, Bearish and Bottoming Process. For all the four stages, a different method is required. Following are some of the most important factors which impact price movement of a particular stock:

- Where the market is going? Is it favouring Bulls or Bear or it is neutral and range bound?
- Check the pricing of stocks, have they become too expensive or still cheaper to own?
- Look for industry trends, sometime gold will shine someday any other metal will glitter.
- How many companies are in queue to go public?
- Results and direction set by those.
- Are people overselling? Are there too many short positions?
- What is put call ratio and VIX?

In the upcoming text of the book, we will talk about the trading strategies which shall take care of the above factors and let the trader learn about how to make profits from the prevailing situation.

In the book we would not like to talk heavy or speak like some big guns of the markets using technical words to preach you. Rather we will discuss some types of easy-to-use swing trading strategies, when to implement and how to match the strategy with the prevailing market conditions. We will let certain charts also speak about the swing trading strategies and show us certain examples about winning trades.

The stoploss is the most important part of any trading strategy, to validate it, let me quote a fantastic example. In the year 2000 a very reputed magazine "Fortune" came up with a list 10 stocks which you can buy and take long long nap. After so many years out of 10 stocks 9 are in red and the best performing is up only 24%. So, it always good to buy the best ones but sticking to those emotionally is not a trait of a good trader. I consider Buy and hold as Buy and hope.

Remember if you don't keep your losses under control than recovery will be very tough for them, most investors get this maths wrong and keep waiting for a recovery even when there is no hope.

Remember:

1. 10% loss needs an 11.3% gain
2. 50% loss needs a 100% gain
3. 95% loss needs a 1900% gain to break even

So, let's begin the journey.....

STRATEGY 1

THE BIG BANG- TRADING THE ACTIVE ONES, THE VOLUME THEORY

A stock is usually tracked for two things, the first important thing is Price and the other most important thing is the Volume of the share. Price is always tracked but a trader must understand that volume is equally important. Volume in a share reflects the level of interest being taken by the small as well as large traders. So it is always important to pay attention on how much volume is being traded in a stock every day. Volumes helps to track what big institutions are doing.

The ground level strategy

1. Daily price gain must be over 5%, anything less than this will not indicate a volume blast in the share.

2. The price of share being traded must be Rs. 300 minimum.

3. As we are talking about a volume strategy, volume itself is the most important indicator for a share. We should look for a minimum 10X of daily average and for sure it must be more than the previous day volume.

4. Breakout is a very important signal, if the share is getting out of recent consolidation then it's a sure shot buy.

5. Only volume tracking is not enough we must track the reason behind it also, there can be several reasons for this event. For Banks, interest rates reduction is probably the best reason to rejoice and for steel industry, raising the import subsidy is a great trigger.

6. The broader market or at least the large indices like NIFTY and SENSEX must be in an uptrend.

Remember that whatever glitters is not always gold, if we speak about trading volumes Vodafone and Yes Bank most of the time tops the charts but as per our general principal, we do not trade stocks below Rs. 300. So avoid these types of stocks.

Base mindset -

Whenever we see huge volume breakout in the share like 10X of daily average, it must be understood as a big event, if you track the incident properly you will find some strong background story which will works as a catapult for earning of a stock and the earnings are for sure about to enter in a re-rating zone. It is a fantastic swing trade opportunity as well as a firm indication of the continuation of price moving upwards. Most of the time you will see stock moving 25 to 75 percent in coming days when the volume blast has happened in a stock. The series of investment announcement in JIO Platforms in year 2020 has been one of such kind of event for Reliance Industries limited, it put the share in a re-rating zone and we all witnessed the performance going forward.

This kind of events happens at least 5 times in a good stock provided that the broader market is in confirm uptrend and the news behind the volume blast is so strong that it has provided a re-rating to the stock.

One caveat which the trader must always keep is that there are a lot of false alarms, for example de-mergers, stock splits etc. these kinds of events are good to trade randomly but even if there is a large volume breakout practically no earning re-rating is seen.

Big volume moves itself is not a very sufficient parameter for stock to be in a good swing trade opportunity. It must be supported by factors like a sure shot market uptrend.

Those stocks which are not in very high float are a good trading opportunity for this trading strategy, as soon as the volumes hit the roof a lot of traders are attracted towards the stock and for sure no one wants to miss an opportunity to own the stock because the perception gets built about stock moving further.

Look for the place to enter

It is a very strategic call to buy the volume shakers from the street as we know that a lot of false alarms are there which gets the investor trapped in a bad stock and further to lose money. Have an eye for 60 minute candle or daily candle to take a swing trade. The big-volume range expansion could have an immediate continuation and remain in play for several weeks after a big breakout. It can also be followed by a 2.5 day to 21 day sideways consolidation or price pullback to a moving average (10, 20 or 50-day EMAs) before there is another leg higher.

The stoploss- yes it's the most important part!

Under this strategy if you have identified a right stock on given parameters than you have an advantage of having a steep stoploss, a trader can have the stoploss at the base he bought or 7 to 8% below the buying level. Here stop loss of 8% is kept as in these cases big immediate momentum can come and we don't want to miss it due to small shake out. If you are an absolute beginner then stop loss can be of 4-5% as well.

Look at the quantity and risk capital

These kind of stocks can move very differently from what you have expected, engaging a huge capital in not required. A trader must not risk more than 0.5%-1% capital as a stop loss. For example if your capital is 1 lakh Rs and you invested 10% in this strategy that is 10,000 Rs and your stop loss is 8% which in Rs term will be 10000 Rs*8%=800 Rs, so you are risking 0.8% of your capital in this particular trade.

Exit at the right point

A trader must look for minimum 3 to 1 big 10 to 1 or even 20 to 1, reward to risk trades. In case of having positions in green a trader can sell half of the position engaged in next 2.5 to 5 days and rest can be sold when a stock closes below a 10, 20 or 50-day EMA.

What is it all about!

A trader must always keep it as a learning that sometime he can go wrong and this sometime can be even 50% time even in roaring bull market, the mistake can be from identifying a wrong stock or misunderstanding the market trend. Sometime the trader gets trapped and have to book losses. So, booking losses is not a bad thing, keep a strong commitment towards your stoploss and adhere to it in any case.

As we know there are a lot of false alarms also, one such scenario is always there for banking stocks when rate cuts are announced. As soon as a surprise rate cut is announced traders gets active and at least the large cap Banking and NBFC stocks gets volume attention. Gradually when market sees that the rate cut is about to create a high inflationary scenario the stocks starts getting cool down and those who took position on the basis of volume breakout gets trapped. There are solutions also to this problem if you get trapped, either cut your losses at an early stage or look for short selling ideas. Remember, it's a wonderful capital protection idea to keep a stoploss, holding a loss position is never a good thing to do.

Always keep searching for volume breakouts but keep it attached with other aspects, standalone volume thing most of the time is just a trading trap which takes the investor along with it and at a later stage he regrets holding it. A trader must not become emotional with the stock bought under this or any strategy, we must know that the markets are there to make money and not to stick to stocks.

Always keep a check on following points:

1. There must be restriction on total capital you are ready to lose in stock, I suggest not to risk more than .5 to 1% of total capital. Here .5% to 1% is the capital lost if stop loss is hit.
2. If the stock goes up further, is it advisable to average on the way up not on the way down. If you are doing

average up than there must be a strict revised trailing stoploss.

3. The stock you purchased, is it the only one available in the market? The answer is a big NO, there are many numbers of stocks available in broader market which keeps showing signs of volume breakout. Trader must get rid of the current one and get into the better ones all the time.

Always remember that making mistake is not a bad thing but taking that mistake together for years is a real bad idea! Making a mistake is ok, but not accepting your mistake is a bigger mistake.

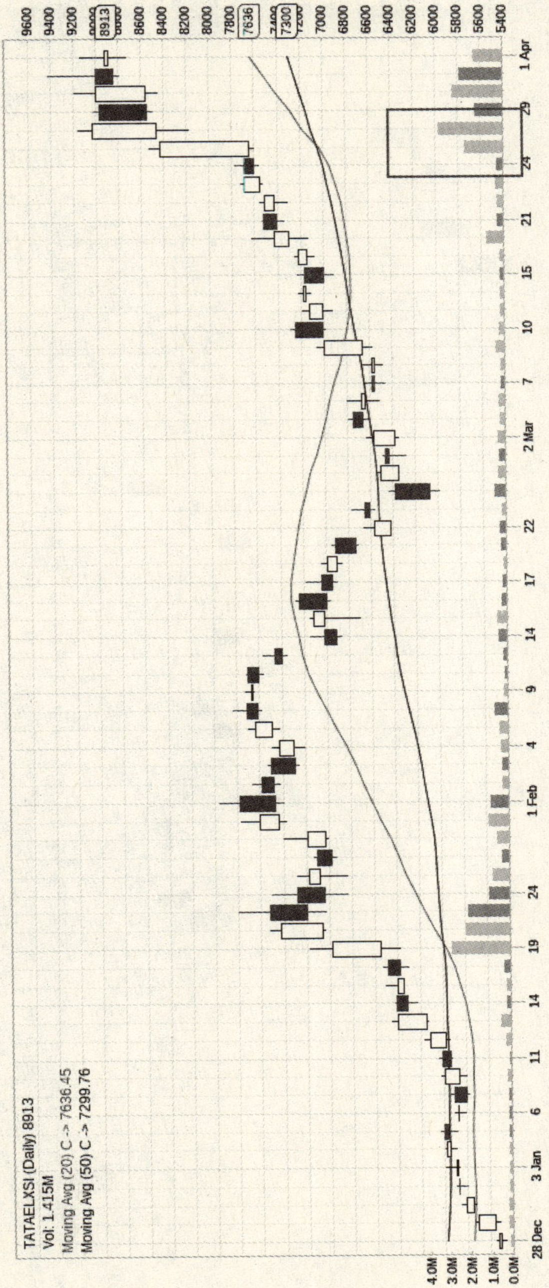
TATAELXSI (Daily) 8913
Vol: 1.415M
Moving Avg (20) C -> 7636.45
Moving Avg (50) C -> 7299.76

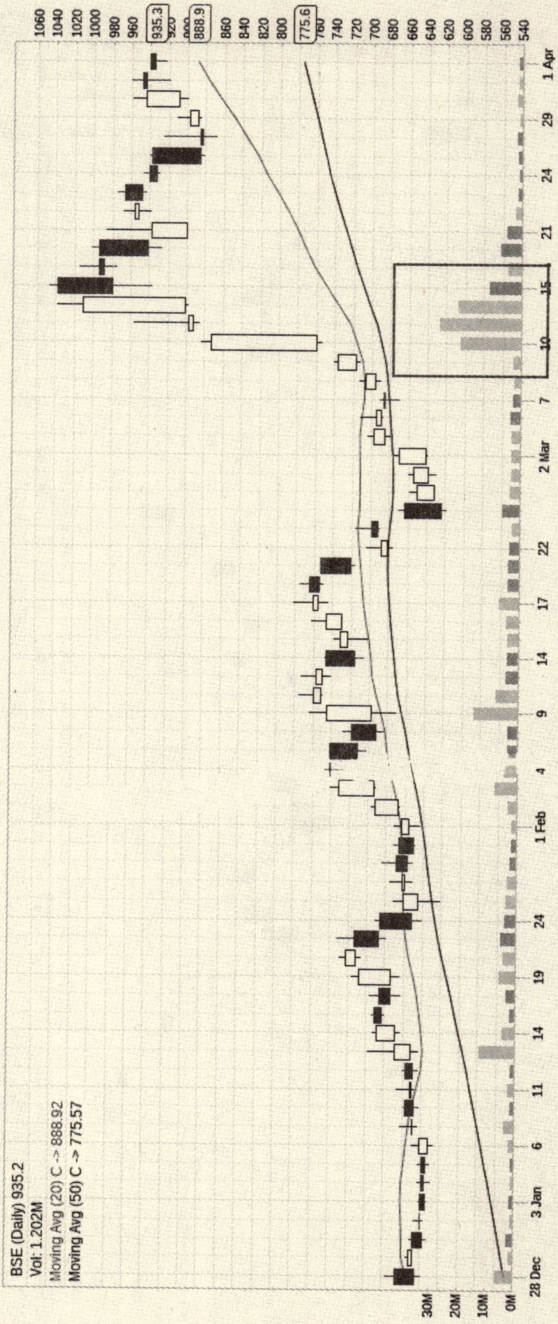
BSE (Daily) 935.2
Vol: 1.202M
Moving Avg (20) C -> 888.92
Moving Avg (50) C -> 775.57
935.3
888.9
775.6
28 Dec
3 Jan
1 Feb
2 Mar
1 Apr
30M
20M
10M
0M

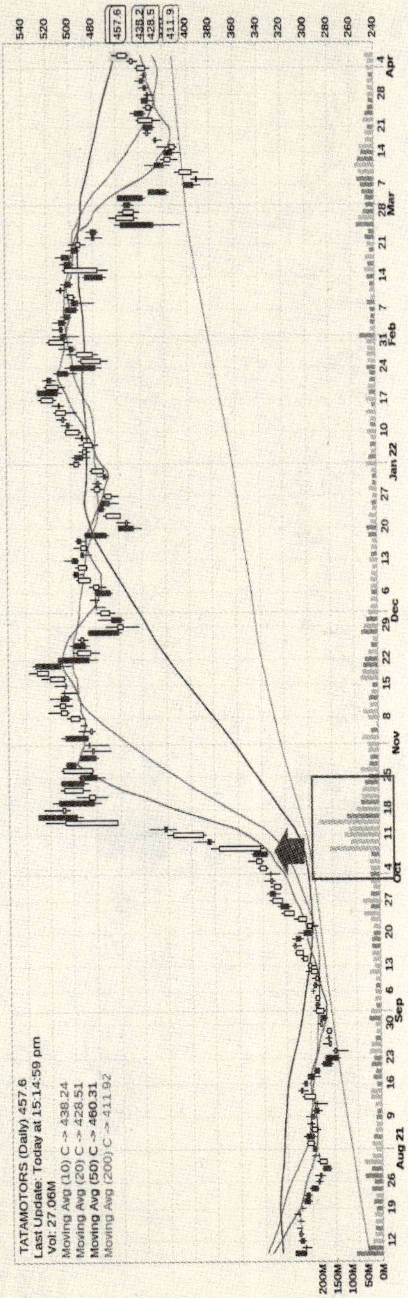
TATAMOTORS (Daily) 457.6
Last Update: Today at 15:14:59 pm
Vol: 27.06M
Moving Avg (10) C -> 438.24
Moving Avg (20) C -> 428.51
Moving Avg (50) C -> 460.31
Moving Avg (200) C -> 411.92
457.6
438.2
428.5
411.9
540
520
500
480
400
380
360
340
320
300
280
260
240
200M
150M
100M
50M
0M
12
19
26
Aug 21
9
16
23
30
Sep
6
13
20
27
4
Oct
11
18
25
Nov
8
15
22
29
Dec
6
13
20
27
Jan 22
10
17
24
31
Feb
7
14
21
28
Mar
7
14
21
28
4
Apr

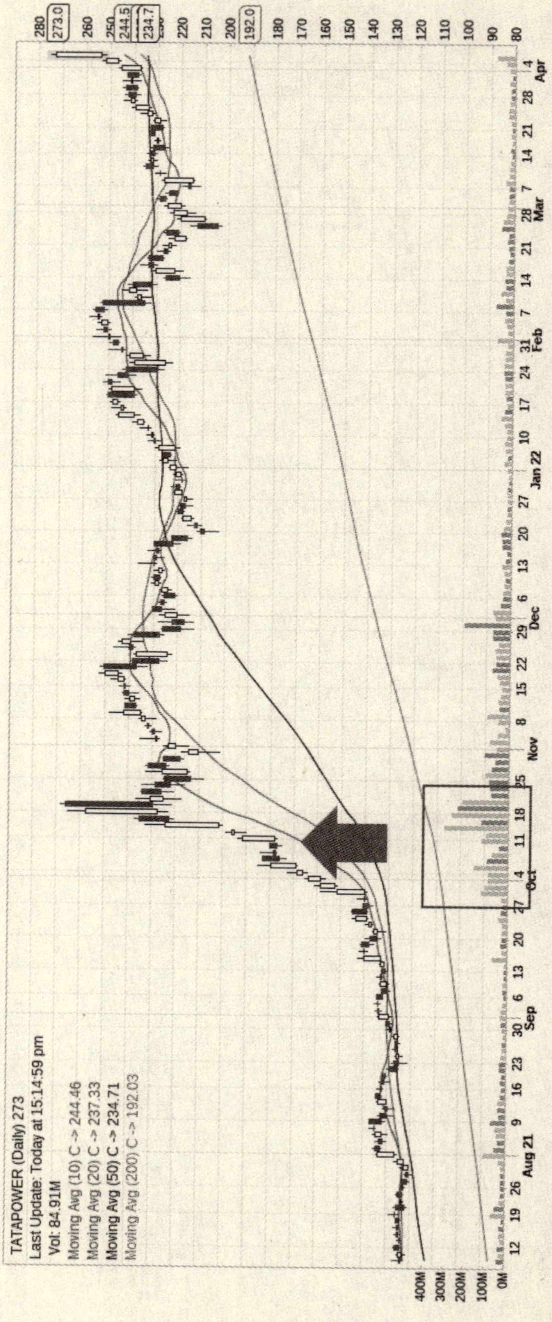
TATAPOWER (Daily) 273
Last Update: Today at 15:14:59 pm
Vol: 84.91M
Moving Avg (10) C -> 244.46
Moving Avg (20) C -> 237.33
Moving Avg (50) C -> 234.71
Moving Avg (200) C -> 192.03

STRATEGY 2

Breakout Trades – When the Stock Breaks the Range

In a general Bull market when the market and stocks are in uptrend it is not advisable to search for shorts in market rather most of the time, we should look for buy trades and make money out of the Bull Trend itself. But it always remains a question how and when to enter a stock, summarily there are three basic ways to enter a stock in this situation:

1. When the market has faced some recent consolidation and then shows an upward movement at that time the trader must buy on the breakout day or next day with the stoploss on the level where market consolidated.

2. Buying at a consolidation in expectation of break out is also a great strategy which should be used only in confirm uptrend. Here you will be able to identify the stock early and gains will be larger.

3. When the market is in a pullback condition to a rising 10-day, 20-day or 50-day exponential moving averages. This also becomes a secondary buying point.

Some basics pointers which should majorly be fulfilled by the stock you are trying to trade -

1. Price of stock must be at least Rs. 300.

2. 3-5% breakout to achieve at new 10 or 20-day high.
3. Average daily traded volume must be more than 1 crore in rupee terms.
4. At this stage indices are like NIFTY and Bank NIFTY must be in a confirmed uptrend. Range contraction is above 10 and 20-day EMAs (Exponential Moving Averages)

The reason behind taking a 3-5% breakout range consolidation to new 10 or 20 day high is that expansions in daily price ranges often start new trends. 3-5% is a big enough move to potentially start a period of upside momentum. This strategy generally works in a Bull Phase of Stock Markets.

Remember that a breakout is not the end of trade rather it's the beginning only, we need to analyse post breakout scenarios very closely, which can be as follows-

1. **Immediate follow through of price and volume-** This is the best thing you want as a trader. This might be one of the after effects of a breakout but it doesn't come always hand in hand. There is very less probability that a stock will keep showing 4-5% uptrend for next 4 to 5 days. After the initial break-out most of the stocks become tricky to trade and provide for intra-day pullbacks which keeps bothering those trading intraday. But as a swing trader you must carefully use these as buying opportunity.
2. **A narrow range consolidation-** Its keeps the stock a bit stronger as this stage will be witnessed generally at the upper part of the breakout day range. Mostly it may continue its upward rally after 2.5 days consolidation.
3. **Giving time tight-range consolidation-** The stock could pull back to a rising 10 days moving average or even 20 or 50 day moving average especially when you are trading

blue chips. Once it has spent time here, it will look for a further run.

4. **Not Sustaining the breakout or in "The Stock Fails to Perform"**- sometime the breakouts proves to be a myth, it just works as a mirage and after getting consolidated it heads towards lower territory and does not make money for traders. Stop loss need to be applied.

To make most of breakout trend a trader must take care of understanding Industry trend and general market momentum. If it collates well with the market then a good trade is all yours.

The ground level strategy

Even in roaring bull markets like we saw from 2003 to 2008 every stock does not go up in straight line around 80% of time is spent in just hovering around a price and building a consolidation before it breaks out. So, always keep an eye on this pre-breakout movements. Bull market doesn't mean that your stock will rise each and every day.

Base mindset

Always remember that breakout doesn't work in a range bound or corrective market, you need at least a Bull Market if not a Super Bull Market.

To confirm about a breakout we need to keep a close eye on the major market averages like NIFTY, Mid-cap and Small-Cap, For instance if Small caps (Small cap Index), mid-caps (Midcap Index), and large caps (NIFTY) are trading above their 50-day moving averages. Also, it helps if small caps (Small cap Index) is trading above its 10/20 day EMA.

Speaking a bit contradictory to what we discussed above is that in some phases of bear markets the stocks will give opportunities in terms of break-outs. We may call those phase as mini bull markets or a correction in Bear Markets. We must learn how to track it. These kind of trend reversals are very usual even in weakest of the bear markets.

Bharti Airtel (in 2021-22) is another good example here, due to pricing pressure in the entire telecom sector for good amount of time it spent in a rigid range and when the market became better it started working and did not feel shy in even crossing Rs 750/- mark immediately.

Look for the place to enter

The trader should buy on the day when there is a break out of more than 3-5% on a particular day and at the same time goes towards fresh 10 or 20 day high.

The stoploss- yes it's the most important part!

Put your stoploss around one percent below the lows of entry day. It is a good stoploss while trading with this strategy another point of the stoploss is around the level below 10/20 day EMA (exponential moving average).

Look at the quantity and risk capital

Risk of capital in breakout trade is usually 0.5% - 1%. On Rs.1 Crore trading capital, 0.5% risk is 50,000 and 1% risk is 1, 00,000. Let's say you want to buy a share at Rs.460 with a stop at Rs.425. Your risk per share is Rs.35. We divide the total risk per idea of 50,000 over the risk per share of Rs.35 to get the number of shares we can afford to buy. In this case, 1,428 shares. The total capital allocation would be: 1428 * Rs.460= Rs.6,56,880 which is about 6.56% of your capital.

Exit at the right point

We are not there to stay forever in the position taken here so in order to make profits we need to devise a plan to exit the stock, In general we sell half 2.5 to 5 trading days after your entry. Pending quantity can be sold and trail to 10/20 day EMA on closing basis.

What is it all about!

1. As we discuss in the initial pages that same strategy shall not work in all the type of markets and on the other hand every strategy will not work in a single phase of market. For, Example breakout trading strategy will earn for you in Bull market. On the other hand if the markets are directionless, this strategy is not going to work. A trader must understand that he must try to find out the strategy which best suits in current market scenarios and if he is uncertain then he must sit on the side lines and try to search for the right opportunity.

2. We all are humans and we have limitations, remember market is always right and we may be right or wrong in our opinion about market. With our experience even if we go right 50% time while trading in market one must feel blessed. Always remember that a trader must not try to be right always. Rather he must try to make most of it when there are initial signals of being right. If you realise that your strategy is not going the way you wanted to, Book a loss and search for a next one. Don't get emotional

with a trade. Let's talk about Jim Simmons here. The mathematician and a wonder of the stock markets who made millions out of it, even his success ratio was not more than 51%. Notably his average holding period of a stock was only 2 days, seems like he always made the most out the market. So, never try be right every time, just try to make big money when you are right. How you know that you may be wrong? Very simple when your stock come down to a particular percentage point from your buy price there are high chances you may be wrong.

3. One thing which is very common with new investors is "Beginner's Luck". Which means that at initial trades a trader will always earn. This is where expectations start getting developed. The trader considers that every day will be same and stocks will start giving him bread and butter. Even if new investor does not use stop loss mostly price come back to his buy level or even above his buy price. It doesn't happen so every time. You must learn that it's very challenging to earn in the markets and you must try to keep the loss making trades at minimum and profit making trades at maximum number. Twenty percent of your trades will account for most of your profits. The rest should be small wins and losses that cancel each other out.

4. Everyone wants to become rich at earliest which is not a bad thing but having logics in place are very important. Desire and Greed have a very thin line in between. To make large money in stock markets a trader has to essentially trade large and that's the first part of a big mistake. Small time traders take big positions in most of the speculative stocks and get overleveraged. This thing works well when the market goes in a single direction but as soon as the

market changes its track the trader starts losing money that time. First half of Calendar year 2008 saw a lot of traders going bankrupt because for the first time in 5 years the market took a halt from a roaring Global Bull Run. Remember, you should never put more than 15% of your capital in a single stock while you swing trade. More recently people were so optimistic about market standing tall on Jan-Feb-March 2020 when the COVID wave was at its initial stage. Lot of traders were too reluctant in selling and when market finally made its bottom on 23 march 2020 most investors was unable to buy they were just licking their wounds.

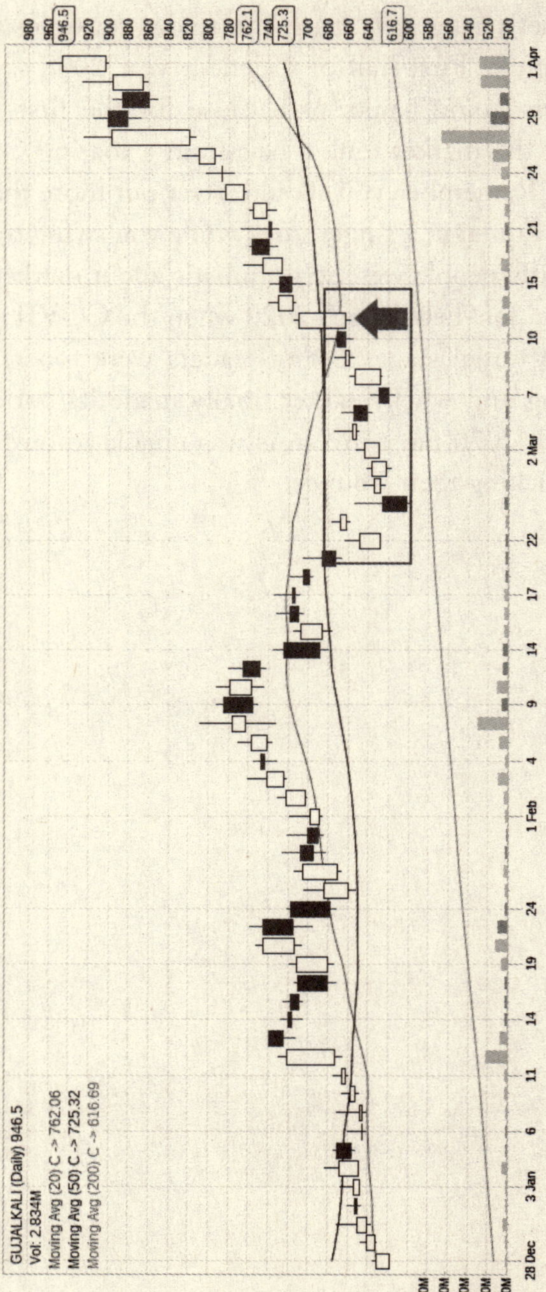
GUJALKALI (Daily) 946.5
Vol: 2.834M
Moving Avg (20) C -> 762.06
Moving Avg (50) C -> 725.32
Moving Avg (200) C -> 616.69
28 Dec
3 Jan
6
11
14
19
24
1 Feb
4
9
14
17
22
2 Mar
7
10
15
21
24
29
1 Apr
980
960
946.5
920
900
880
860
840
820
800
780
762.1
740
725.3
700
680
660
640
616.7
600
580
560
540
520
500
8.0M
6.0M
4.0M
2.0M
0.0M

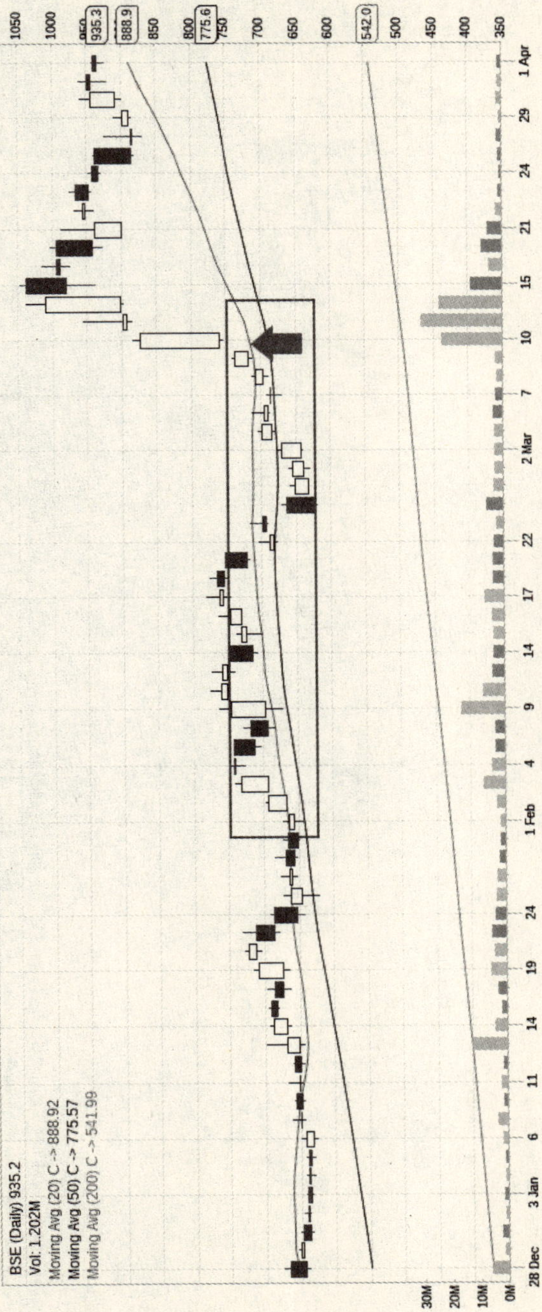
BSE (Daily) 935.2
Vol: 1.202M
Moving Avg (20) C -> 888.92
Moving Avg (50) C -> 775.57
Moving Avg (200) C -> 541.99
1050
1000
935.3
888.9
850
800
775.6
750
700
650
600
542.0
500
450
400
350
30M
20M
10M
0M
28 Dec
3 Jan
6
11
14
19
24
1 Feb
4
9
14
17
22
2 Mar
7
10
15
21
24
29
1 Apr

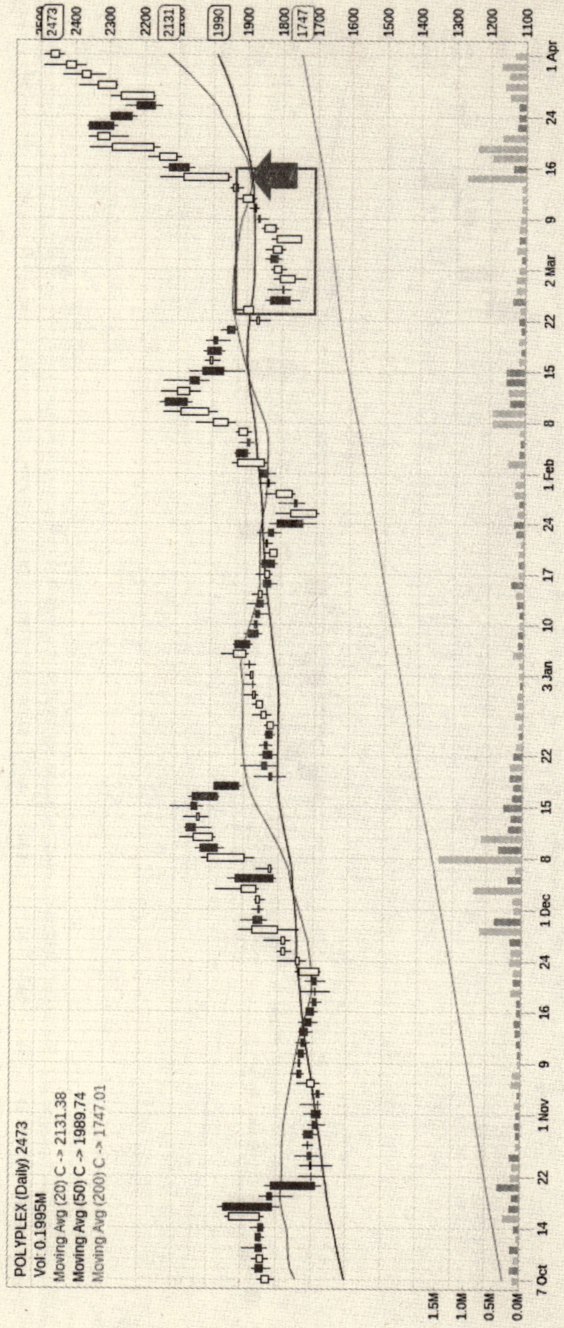
POLYPLEX (Daily) 2473
Vol: 0.1995M
Moving Avg (20) C -> 2131.38
Moving Avg (50) C -> 1989.74
Moving Avg (200) C -> 1747.01

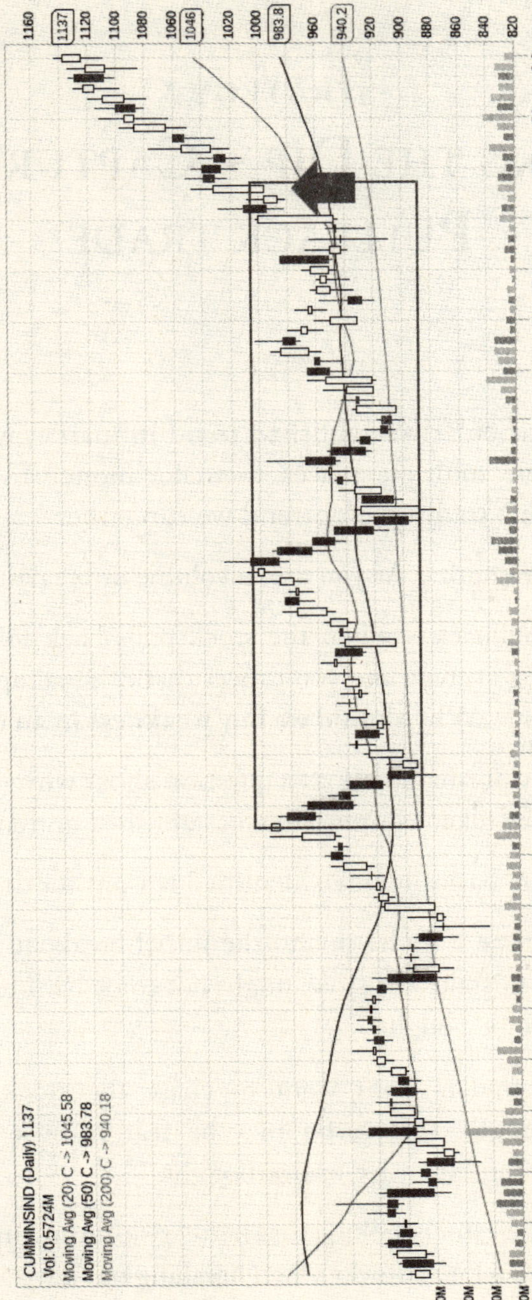
CUMMINSIND (Daily) 1137
Vol: 0.5724M
Moving Avg (20) C -> 1045.58
Moving Avg (50) C -> 983.78
Moving Avg (200) C -> 940.18

STRATEGY 3

Buying the Dip – Capturing a Pullback trade

Any particularly established trend in market will always provide multiple places to make money for a swing trader. While trading in uptrend we can either

1. Buy strength – As you use in volume or breakout strategy.
2. Buy pullback – when the stock pulls back to some key moving average and you expect that original uptrend will continue. **Why should we buy weakness in an uptrend?**

It is very normal to ask as a question about why a particular trade must be taken contrary to an established uptrend?

There are basically three identified reasons for doing so:

1. Sometime a trader misses the initial breakout and it is a costly mistake, the stock might not come back to the same level to be bought.
2. Most traders don't want to chase the stock and buy in strength, the reason may be fear because of stocks becoming expensive or overbought.
3. If the investor is looking for a better risk/reward mechanism because a lot of stocks when breaking out have a tendency to pullback temporarily

Sometime it's good to catch the falling knife if you know the art of doing so. Buying the dips is simple strategy of finding those stocks which are oversold and a position for a turnaround can be taken in those. Every oversold stock bounces for some time and we need to identify it for a swing trade. Here, a swing trader essentially not looking for the nadir of a stock's price rather he is looking for a comfortable place to enter make some decent gains.

The ground strategy

1. To implement this strategy we are looking for those stocks which are up more than 20% in the past 30 days or more than 30% in the past 90 days or more than 50% in the past 180 days. This means that we buy on pullbacks only sound stocks have strong momentum.

2. Look for some consolidation in the stock – these consolidations can be of time or price. For time it will be in sideways moves and for price it will move around 10, 20 or 50-day exponential moving averages.

3. Here, we are strictly looking for those stocks which are more than Rs. 300 in terms of pricing.

4. Minimum trading volume in stock is at least Rs. 1 crore per day.

Look at your path

Though here we are adopting a strategy to buy weakness in stocks but we must not be in a mood to play blind, we must not get up in the morning and buy any weakness in an uptrend. Remember, there are factors to look upon. Few important ones are following:

1. We need to make sure that the major market composition and broader market is in uptrend and we are not trading any dead-cat bounce.

2. High momentum stocks are preferred which belongs to market favourite industries. Seasonal ones will not make much money for a trader.

3. A trader may buy to pullback which is towards a rising 10 or 20 or 50 day moving average provided stock is showing low volume near these moving average. In other words, we buy pullbacks if it is happening with low volumes.

4. As a trader you may not only look for a pullback which is towards a random 10 or 20 or 50-day moving average but you must do some wait and watch until the trend gets confirmed. Usually a 3-5% bounce near a stock's 10 or 20 or 50-day EMAs (exponential moving averages) is good signal to work on it

5. Look for the stocks or indices which are in a long term uptrend and have traced back to 50 day EMA, this presents an opportunity to buy the stock for a swing trade. Here stock can retrace to 50-day exponential moving average and can even go down for intraday day and bounces back the same day or stock can close below 50- day EMA with lower volume than earlier days and then the next day stock bounces back above its 50 EMA line. This strategy is a great potential opportunity for a swing trader. The 50-day is a higher probability dip buy signal.

While taking care of all of the factors mentioned above we must still keep a clear cut understanding that every trade will not make money and there will be losing trades also. So, don't worry about the losses and if you are doing it right your winning trades will cover everything you lost.

The 50-day moving average dip-buying parameters

1. Price bounces near the 50 day EMA and closes above it, price moves below the 50-day EMA intraday but closes back above it, or price closes below the 50-day line but next day closes above it.
2. Profit target could be in the range of 6-10 %.
3. Example of Deepak Nitrite repeatedly bouncing off the 50-day EMA in 2020-21.

How the strategy works?

First of all we need to understand that stock which are in confirmed momentum are market favourites, you will always see price and volume actions in these ones as they are preferred by the biggies of industry. There are long term buyers which will keep the stocks up for at least few months. They are not looking to flip a stock for a 50 % gain. It takes time to make some long term positions on the stock. We must understand that large investors are not looking to invest for a very short term, their strategy is to stick to the market.

Sometimes, stock bounces above their rising 10 or 20 and 50-day moving averages which is a behaviour against our strategy. It generally happens because some section of trader and investors considers that the stock is going to perform in near term, In addition, they start working and investing on it and consider it as low risk entry point. Therefore the stock gets into a mini uptrend, which can be used by swing trader.

At other times, stocks even work in a different style, share touches their moving averages with very thin volumes, let people cut their positions and then the stocks come back above their 10/20/50 EMA. Such situation is also a strong signal that market does not work singularly, it has its own method of working.

When to trade with this strategy?

This strategy must be adopted in purely confirmed uptrend, which simply means that the stocks must be above its 50 DMA and this 50 DMA must be above its 200 DMA. The other major indices which are to be tracked within are NIFTY and Bank NIFTY. Sometime even indices like small cap and mid cap also indicates good.

If a trader is considering to trade by understanding that the trend is going to continue it must always identify high momentum stocks. Look for industry leaders or blue chips only as these always have a high probability of breaking through a tight consolidation range over the period of time.

Sometime it happens that dips and bounces stops working even in very strong stocks, as a trader you must read the signal, the market is not behaving as it used to be. The market does not change its uptrend to a correction stage like that only, there must be a strong reason behind it. At this stage the market behaves in a confused manner, it selects a range for itself and keeps running around it. Following are two good strategies to adopt at this stage-

1. Look for an industry that is behaving contra to a trend.
2. If you don't find an industry like that then sit on the side-lines have cash and do the least amount of trade.

Look for the place to enter

1. When you predict the breakout coming again, try to enter in its tight price and low volume trading days, at this particular time the share is not very much noticed by the large ones.

2. Try to have your own list of stocks in which you wish to trade in general. Enter the strongest stocks when those make new 20 day high or even very near to that.

3. Enter a pullback around a rising 10 or 20 or 50-day EMA. While working this strategy you need to keep your stop losses in control.

4. Look for a 3-5% bounce from a rising 10 or 20 or 50-day EMA before you buy the stock. This stage might signal the start of a new run-up.

The stoploss- yes it's the most important part!

You should put your stop at half a percent below the entry day's low or a stock's 10 or 20/50-day EMA.

Look at the quantity and risk capital

Risk is 0.5%- 1% of capital. On a Rs.20 Lakh account, 1% risk means 20,000. If we want to buy a stock at Rs.2300 with a stop at Rs.2200, our risk per share is Rs.100.

We divide our total risk per idea of Rs.20,000 over our risk per share of Rs.100. The result is 200 shares. This is the maximum number of shares we can afford to buy. 200 shares x Rs.2300= Rs.4,60,000.

Rs.4,60,000 is a finely large capital allocation for a 20Lakh account. We must restrict it to 20% of the account, which would be Rs.4,00,000 in this specific case.

Exit at the right point

Around half of the quantity to be sold at 2.5 to 5 days after your entry, sell the rest on a close below a 10/20/50 day EMA. Selling on strength works a lot and it serves every purpose of our swing trading which talks about 8 to 12% of gains from a stock. Profit booking is always done on good days.

What is it all about!

Knowing strength and weakness always allows us to perform better, both in life and stock markets. We must keep studying the past trades and learn from right and wrong things we did. Keep asking few questions to you all the time:

1. The strategy which you took, did it work well in the ongoing market environment? If not, then reconsider it.
2. What was your entry point? Was it a good place to get into stock?
3. Did you work strongly and with full commitment on The stoploss?
4. Did you take full advantage of the trade? Did you make enough money or exited early?
5. The time phase in which you were trading, were you prepared in all manner to do that?

   If answer is negative for any of the above then a trader has to change his strategy.

You need to ask these questions to yourself only and the answers shall also come from your inner self, a close inspection of those answers will keep enlightening you and make your future trades better than ever.

Unlike a trend trader a swing trader is looking for certain signals on charts to ascertain probability of short term momentum based gains. He is not at all looking to enter the stock for a long term even if the trajectory and trend is in a great Bull Phase. As we said in the opening statement that buying dip is like catching a falling knife but you must master the art of it. Look for string signals on chart and chase the trajectory of knife where it is blunt and falling at a slower pace. Catch it on the rightest point and that wait for it to turn for your gains.

Adding to the topic we can say that besides analysing the strategy we must keep studying the stocks also in a very serious manner, keep studying the past performance of the stocks, studying stock with regards to the past performance can give you some great data which can give such winning trade. This exercise can be extremely helpful in getting not good but great trades.

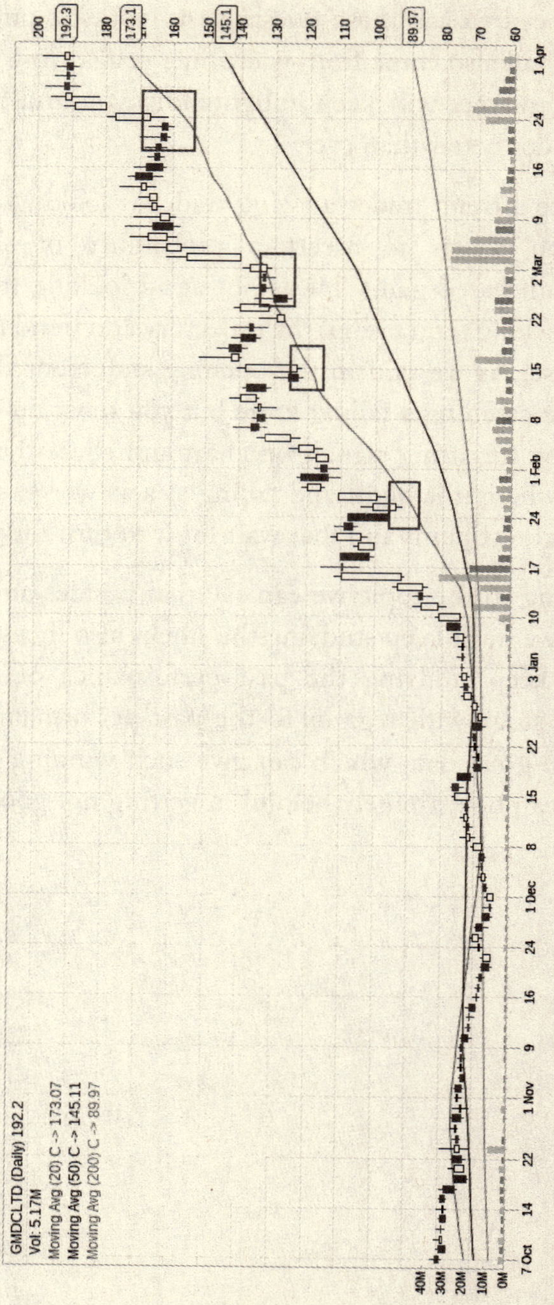
GMDCLTD (Daily) 192.2
Vol: 5.17M
Moving Avg (20) C -> 173.07
Moving Avg (50) C -> 145.11
Moving Avg (200) C -> 89.97
192.3
173.1
145.1
89.97
200
180
160
150
140
130
120
110
100
80
70
60
40M
30M
20M
10M
0M
7 Oct
14
22
1 Nov
9
16
24
1 Dec
8
15
22
3 Jan
10
17
24
1 Feb
8
15
22
2 Mar
9
16
24
1 Apr

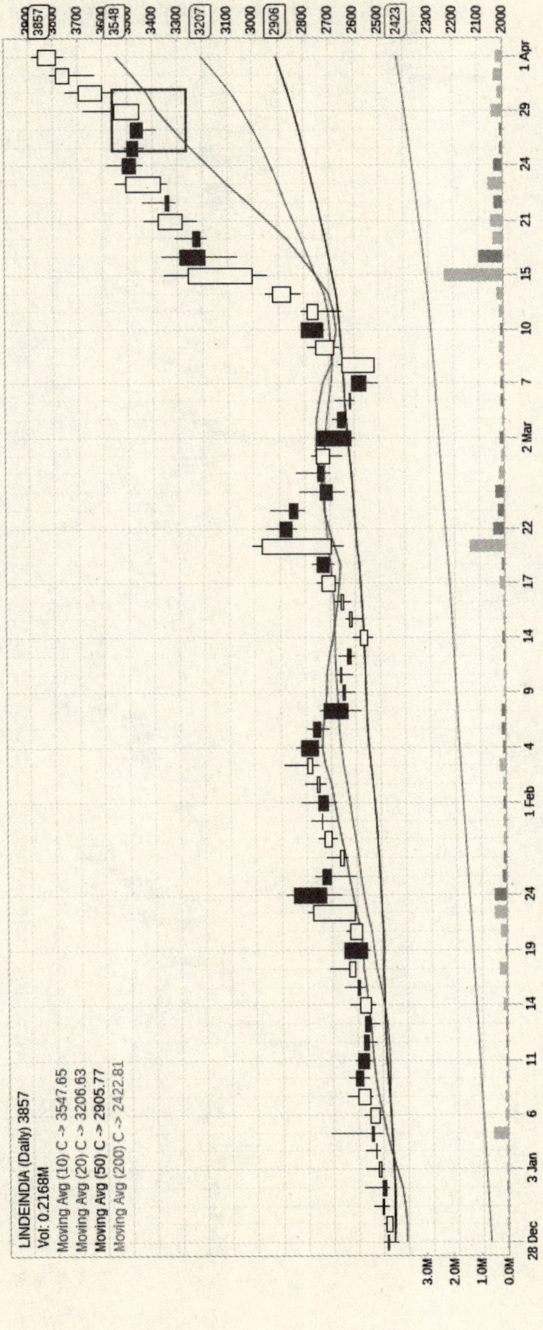
LINDEINDIA (Daily) 3857
Vol: 0.2168M
Moving Avg (10) C -> 3547.65
Moving Avg (20) C -> 3206.63
Moving Avg (50) C -> 2905.77
Moving Avg (200) C -> 2422.81

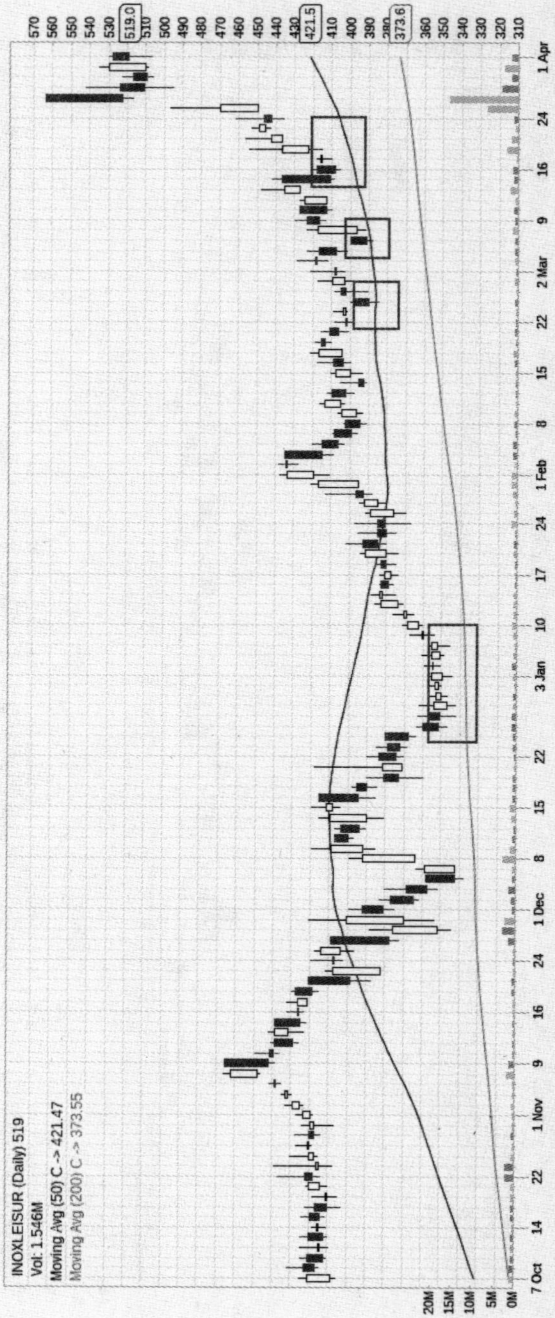
INOXLEISUR (Daily) 519
Vol: 1.546M
Moving Avg (50) C -> 421.47
Moving Avg (200) C -> 373.55

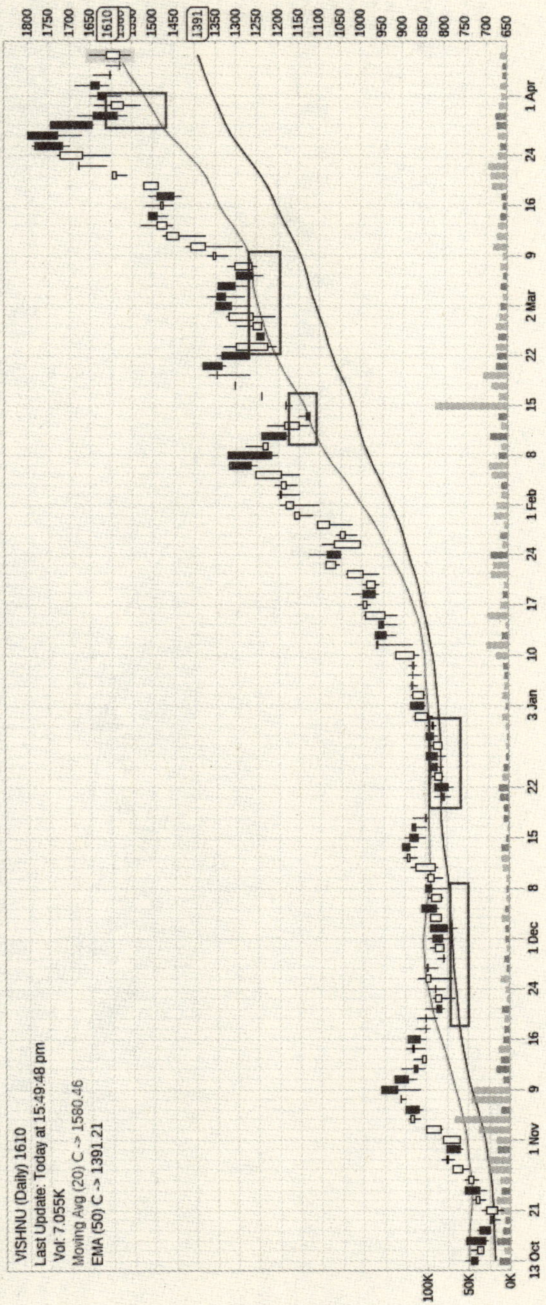
VISHNU (Daily) 1610
Last Update: Today at 15:49:48 pm
Vol: 7.055K
Moving Avg (20) C -> 1580.46
EMA (50) C -> 1391.21

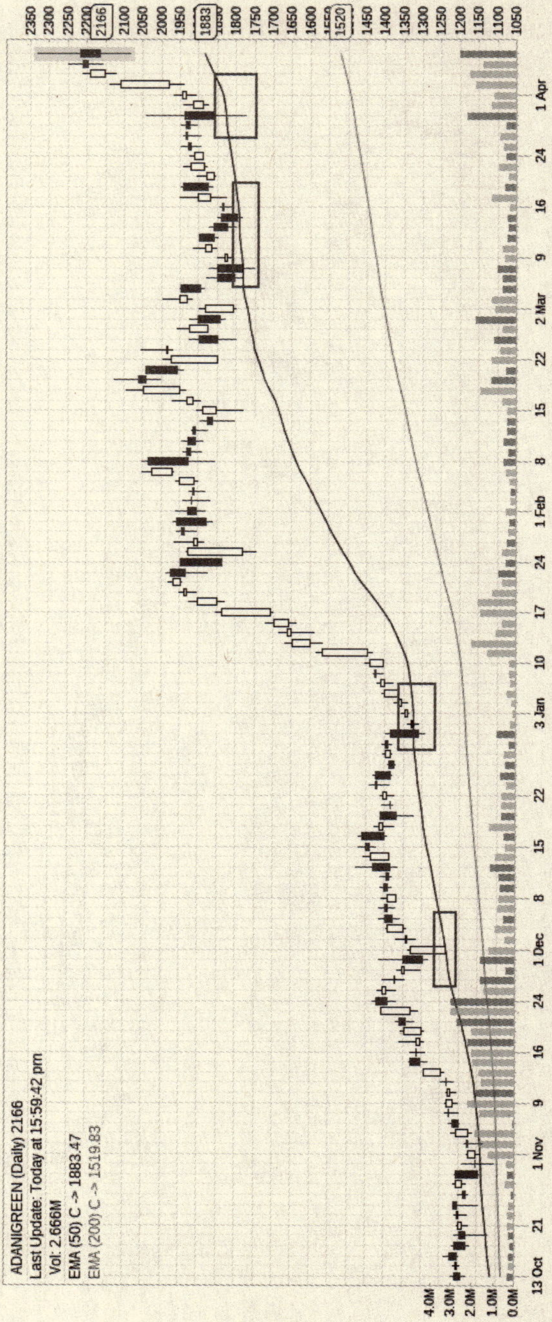
ADANIGREEN (Daily) 2166
Last Update: Today at 15:59:42 pm
Vol: 2.666M
EMA (50) C -> 1883.47
EMA (200) C -> 1519.83

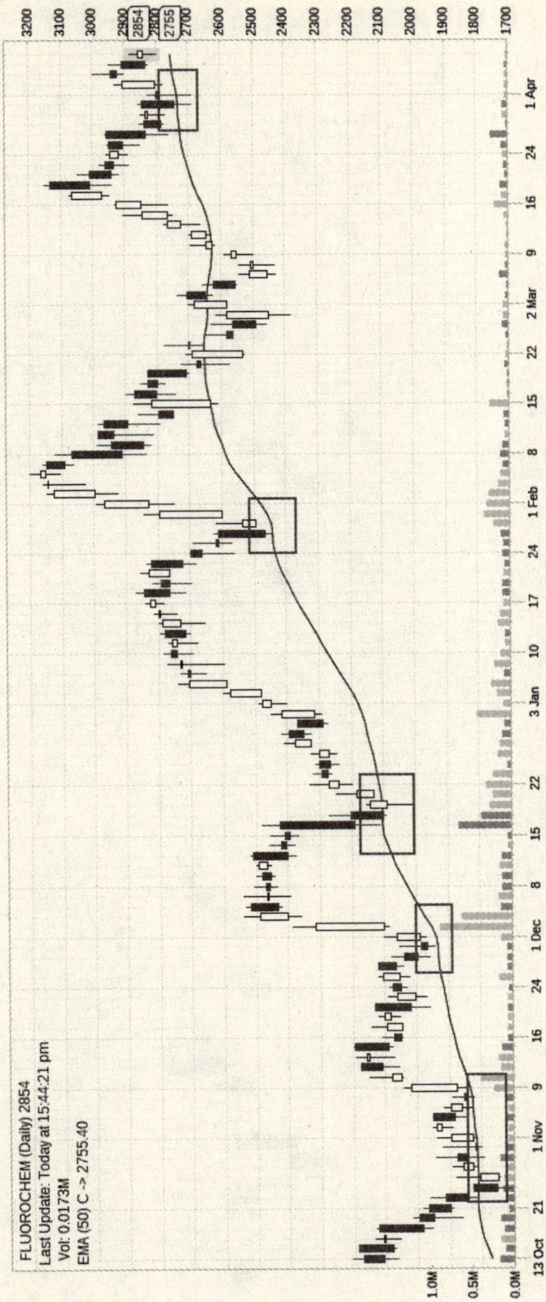
FLUOROCHEM (Daily) 2854
Last Update: Today at 15:44:21 pm
Vol: 0.0173M
EMA (50) C -> 2755.40

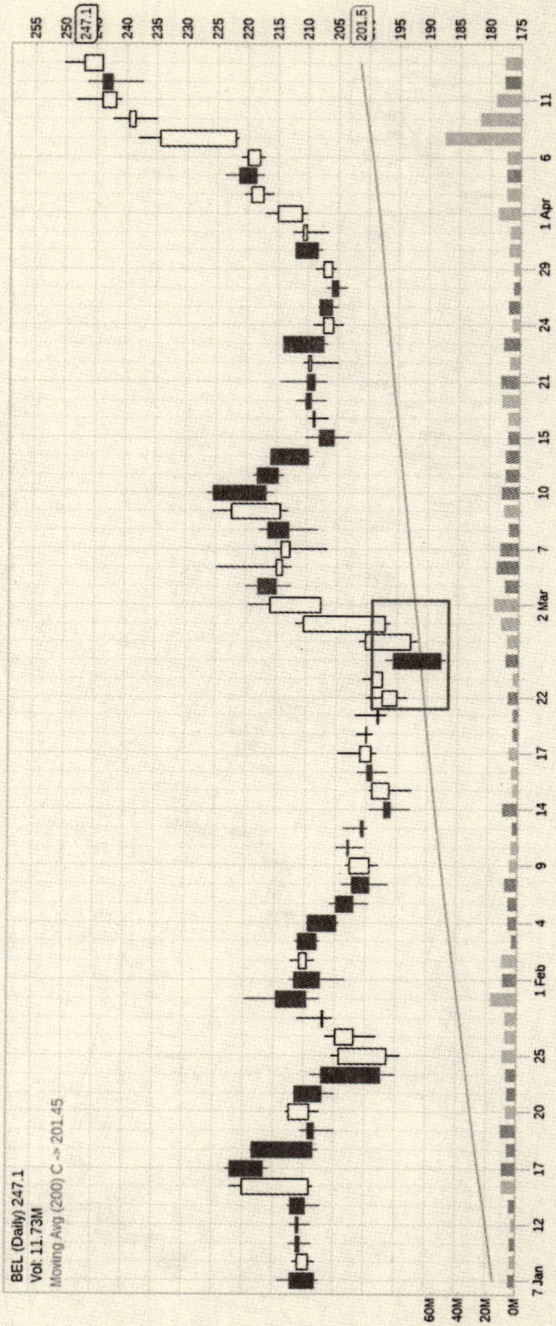
BEL (Daily) 247.1
Vol: 11.73M
Moving Avg (200) C -> 201.45
255
250
247.1
240
235
230
225
220
215
210
205
201.5
195
190
185
180
175
60M
40M
20M
0M
7 Jan
12
17
20
25
1 Feb
4
9
14
17
22
2 Mar
7
10
15
21
24
29
1 Apr
6
11

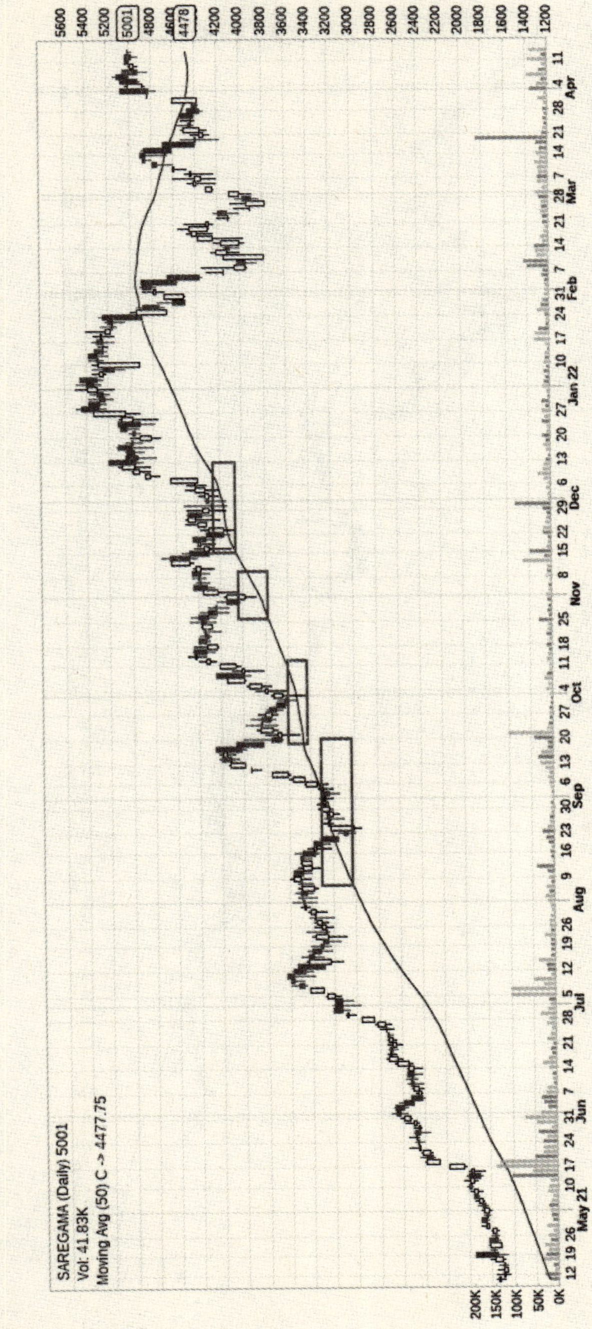
SAREGAMA (Daily) 5001
Vol: 41.83K
Moving Avg (50) C -> 4477.75

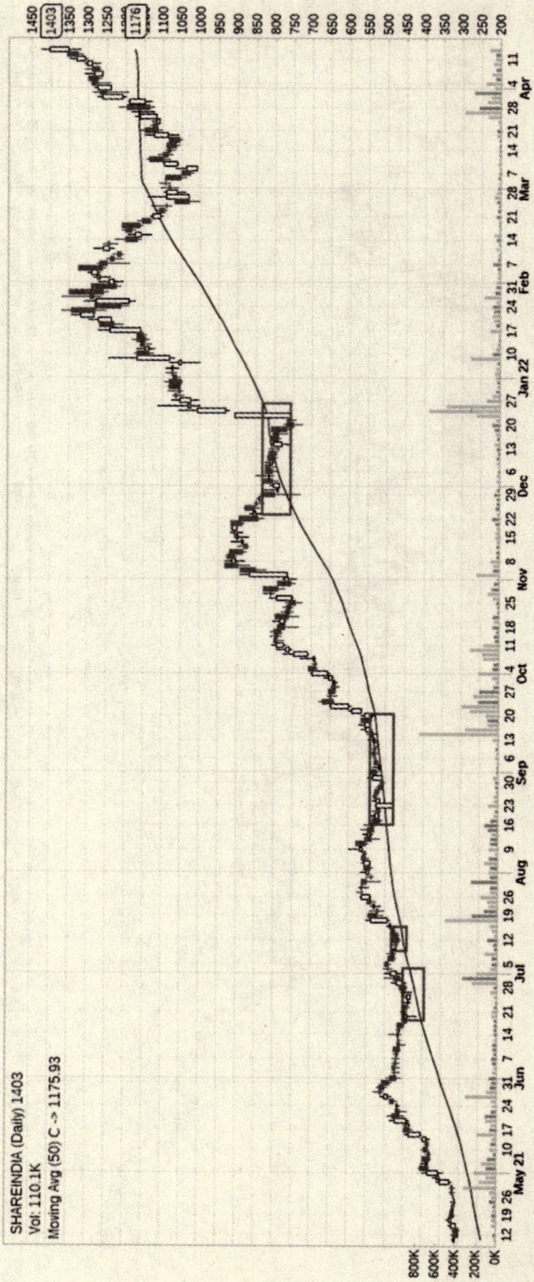
SHAREINDIA (Daily) 1403
Vol: 110.1K
Moving Avg (50) C -> 1175.93

STRATEGY 4

IPO Trading- Make the most of Recent Entrants in Market

As an investor in market we all know how IPOs are floated and how the companies go public, To keep it simple we can say that IPO is an event when company sell its shares to common public, Institutional investors and HNIs. By this event a company's stock goes from being illiquid to liquid and starts getting traded in the secondary market.

IPO is a landmark in any company's lifetime, whether it's a small or a large company or size of a float. In markets like India there is always a lot of appetite for IPO market and every year number of investors getting to IPO market is just growing.

Talking in terms of trading market an IPO is always a talking thing as it has got support from all the groups i.e. common public, Institutional investors and HNIs, especially in a Bull market IPO is "The Thing" to have your attention. Also be it beginner or advanced market player, everyone is excited about IPOs.

The ground level strategy

While trading through IPO strategy, following must be important points to be paid attention on:

1. We must trade in recently listed shares which give priority to those ones which are not more than one year old.
2. Price per share must be at least Rs. 300.
3. Average volume to be Rs. 1 Cr per day.
4. Looking for a breakout which can give around 3 to 5 % of gains, this type of breakout generally comes after a ranged consolidation of 10 to 20%. The market scenario at that time can be of recovering from a recent correction or a real strong bull market.
5. Don't always look for trading at an all-time high but it might be a good thing to do so, in our past experience we have seen that most of the recently listed IPOs moves big time when they are away around 40 to 50% from their all-time high.
6. If the share belongs to the industry which is current flavour of market always helps an IPO trader.
7. Those stocks which are from a segment which are seen with exuberance in market will suit better.

How does an IPO market works?

- Those companies which are recently listed in general have a smaller float as the companies are in growth stage. This float is very easy to work in the market. Large institutional investors play roles of both buyer and seller.
- A lot of HNIs and large funds participate in the IPO market, these funds are not generally "long only" fund and their float starts coming to the market as the objective is to take advantage of IPO momentum and not to stick

for very long term. In Indian market conditions anchor investment tenure in IPO market is also a very important factor.

- On the other hand, in hugely subscribed IPOs a lot of investors and HNIs do not get allotment and due to this they start buying from open market.

A trader must remember that sometime the frenzy of IPO market allows the traders and even long only funds to take a contrarian call. A recent example is Zomato Limited's IPO. A company which is very far from profits came up with IPO and to the market amusement even dividend yield funds applied to it. For sure it was only for listing gains.

While working at IPO we must look for institutional activities very closely, a burning example is the 2008 reliance power IPO where even the Reliance Mutual Funds was shy in applying. We have to always accept that big money is smarter than us, so we just need to follow what big money is doing. Due to recent regulations anchor investment has also become a great data to look at.

A deadly combination-Super growth story, Small caps and a roaring Bull Market!!!

The above mentioned three factors coming together always make a classic IPO Story, those companies which belong to the sectors with high perceived growth story floats IPO in a bull market and comes up with a smaller number of shares to go public always make a great IPO trade. Reason is very simple; every investor wants to get a pie of this growth story and because the supply is very less, demand always outpaces it and the result is a vertical price graph.

Here, we can understand this overall situation with Indian IPO example, as we witnessed a great Bull Market in 2021 and a lot of small and large IPOs hit the market, almost every IPO baring few got great subscription and a created huge frenzy in market. One of those kind of small float IPO was "Latent View Analytics" a data and analytics consulting company which came up with an IPO in Nov 2021, the total issue size was 600 core which was very small compared to the markets, per share issue price was 197 which went upto 700 within three days of listing. Indian markets are full of these kind of IPO stories where the institutional investors and HNIs are ready to take share for a skywalk.

Base mindset

It's always a money-making tool when we trade recently listed IPOs as the momentum is high and float is low. But the grass is always greener on the other side of the fence, lot of cases are there which even after reaching to 100% gains stock goes below issue price in few days. So, it's very important to know when to use this strategy, following points will help you:

- Super bull markets, when all major stock indices like NIFTY and Bank NIFTY are trading above their 20, 50 and 200-day moving averages.
- Just a few days after the stock gets into a correction, generally a 10% decline in the NIFTY 50.

Another important point to remember is that very few companies adventure to go public during market correction timing. Reasons are very simple of this happening. In correction phase of market there are very few takers of IPOs and even shares get lesser valuations when compared to Bull Markets.

Angel and SBI Cards are the best example which got listed on discount due to market correction but performed well later on.

It's always a fantastic opportunity to trade in IPOs when it is launched just before the market corrections. As the market corrections are not ever standing and it takes the share to a temporary downtrend and when the uptrend starts the share starts its Bull Run, Let's understand this with an example. Some of the stocks goes below issue price and even up to 70% corrections is faced by those. For those companies which have a great earning visibility it's a great opportunity to enter.

A company named ICRA limited came up with its public issue of Rs. 85 crore in 2007 with issue price of Rs. 330 per share, The Issue came in March 2007 which was early beginning of a global financial market turmoil. The share went to Rs. 1100/- very soon and that the crash of 2008 hit the market, ICRA came near to its issue price of Rs. 330 and it was a great buying opportunity. Since then it has been in a roaring Bull Phase and while writing this piece the share is trading at around Rs. 4300/- per share. After hitting an all-time high of Rs. 4998/-

Some of the other recent examples of this kind of trade is recently listed IPOs like MTAR, UTI AMC, Route, Ease my trip and Laxmi organic

UTI AMC after reaching to a high of 1200+ traced back to sub 700 levels and got back 1000 Rs. just after the correction got over. Another strong case is of Angel Broking which listed on a discount at around 300 level. Proved itself to be a multi bagger in a Bull Run with almost 5 times returns. Ease my trip went to 350 plus levels where it used to be traded below 100, this all happened within a short span of time just within few months of listing.

Look for the place to enter

Even after the entire fairy tale scenario IPO must not be bought blindly, there are some rules to it. We must look for a contraction which is expected to be followed by a range explosion. For these contraction we need to look at charts very carefully, these could be found very near to all time high or even 52-week low.

In general, there are two ways to enter a stock through IPO strategy

1. One section is to enter after a 3-5% move around the breakout after the consolidation. Consolidation phase is time period where a stock consolidates in a small range for some time.

2. The second place to enter is to when the breakout is very near and charts have started showing signs of this, to do this we must pick those stock which are from the flavoured industry. Initial sign can be in terms of sudden high volumes or more days of upmoves as compared to downmoves.

The stoploss- yes it's the most important part!

If you are buying on the 3-5% breakout day then keep your stoploss at breakout day's low. If bought at the second stage which is buying at early breakout signs stage then your stop should be about 1% below the lows of the established range.

Look at the quantity and risk capital

Around 1% of capital should be risked at most on any recent IPOs. Let's assume that your current trading capital is

20Lakh. Then, 1% risk per trade means Rs.20, 000 risk per Strategy.

If you buy a recent IPO at Rs.2400 per share with a stop at Rs.2200, then you can afford to buy 100 shares. To get to that number, divide your risk per trade of Rs.20, 000 over your risk per share of Rs.200. This means that your capital allocation to this trade is 12% (100 shares * Rs.2400).

If your trade does not work well, you will lose 1% of your capital and if your deal struck well, let's say your stock of interest goes quickly from Rs.2400 to Rs.4000- which is not unusually for hot new IPOs - then you will make Rs.800 per share profit. This is six times your risk per share. Since you risked 1% of your capital, it means that in this case you will add 8% to your annual return.

Exit at the right point

An IPO trade is not a very long term trading strategy, it must be used to make some hot money in the market. 2.5 to 8-day swing trades or 2.5 to 8-week position trades is good trading strategy while trading in an IPO.

Any company has few reasons to get public, some are below mentioned:

1. Raising virtually cost free capital for the future growth.
2. To provide a partial or full exit opportunity to promoters, early investors or employees holding ESOPs.
3. Unlocking the value for company.

If the market is supporting and the company belongs to one of the favourite sectors there will be only buyers in of the shares,

PE expansion to horrendous levels is a general trend in market, those commanding PE of 50 can go up to 120 in very short time. This provides a perfect opportunity to a trader to make money in IPO market. In a roaring bull market people want to buy everything and anything, some of the recent examples are Nazara, MTAR Technology, IRCTC, Route mobile, Happiest Mind and Rosary biotech Etc.

But another part of the story is that this trend does not lasts forever and someday the investors holding a large quantity would like to sell and make windfall gains. That's why a proper exit strategy is very much required while trading in an IPO.

What is it all about!

There are three reasons for learning to trade IPO strategies

1. Their potential gains can be upto 50-100%.
2. The factors involved in the trend can be easily understood even by a layman.
3. Very few companies are in the category of freshly listed IPO at a time, so the trader has to track limited number of stocks.

Sometime we have to compare the IPO market with broader market or major indices. As we discussed earlier that a raging bull marker, small cap issue and hot industry will always provide a great opportunity to trade an IPO. At the same time trading can be done in larger market also but the difference is about opportunity cost. A normal stock will not have momentum to upwards in range of 50 to 100% but a recently listed share shall have the capacity to go to that level. You can make Rs. 100/- in an IPO where you will be able to make Rs. 10/- in general market trades. In recent times especially in Indian market we are seeing a huge frenzy of new IPOs flooding in as the market conditions have been quite favourable and the overall growth momentum is good. In these times it is always better to trade in an IPO than a common stock.

It is very evident that a recent listed IPO will provide trading opportunities for at least first twelve months, so even if you miss the very early part of the momentum you always have a lot of instance to enter into stock and make money out of it.

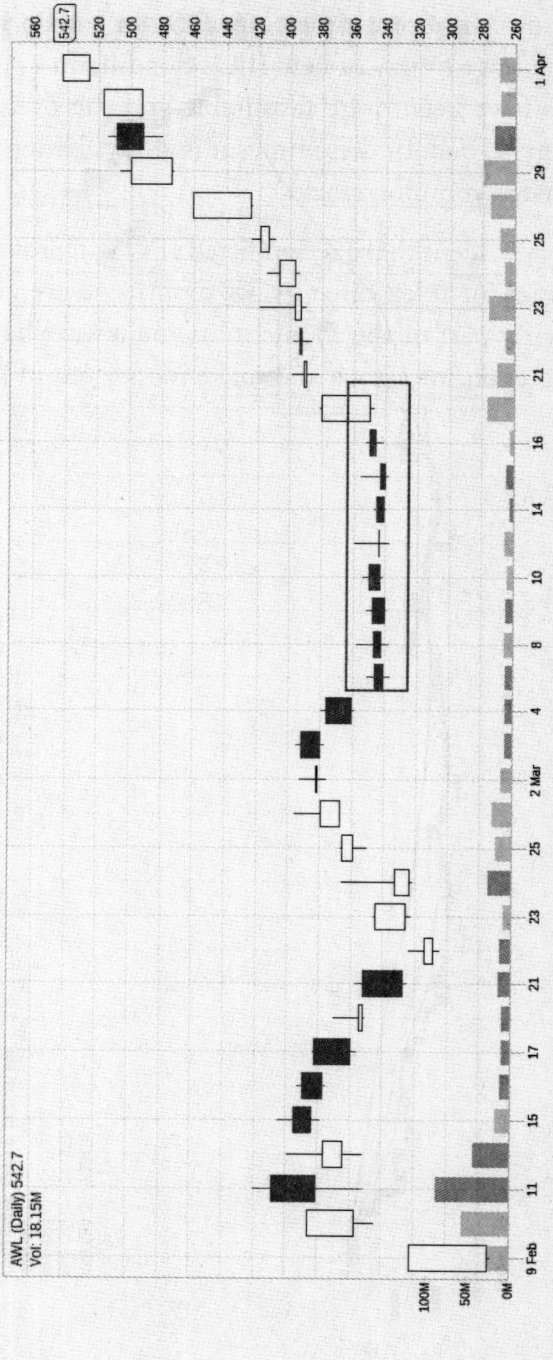
AWL (Daily) 542.7
Vol: 18.15M
560
542.7
520
500
480
460
440
420
400
380
360
340
320
300
280
260
100M
50M
0M
9 Feb
11
15
17
21
23
25
2 Mar
4
8
10
14
16
21
23
25
29
1 Apr

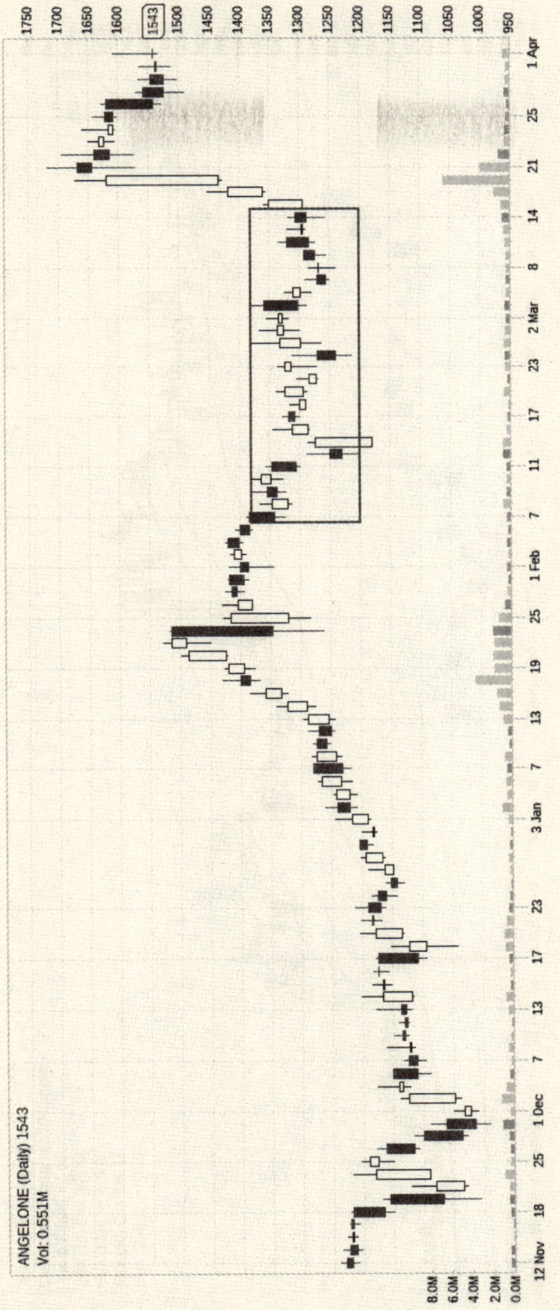
ANGELONE (Daily) 1543
Vol: 0.551M
1750
1700
1650
1600
1543
1500
1450
1400
1350
1300
1250
1200
1150
1100
1050
1000
950
8.0M
6.0M
4.0M
2.0M
0.0M
12 Nov
18
25
1 Dec
7
13
17
23
3 Jan
7
13
19
25
1 Feb
7
11
17
23
2 Mar
8
14
21
25
1 Apr

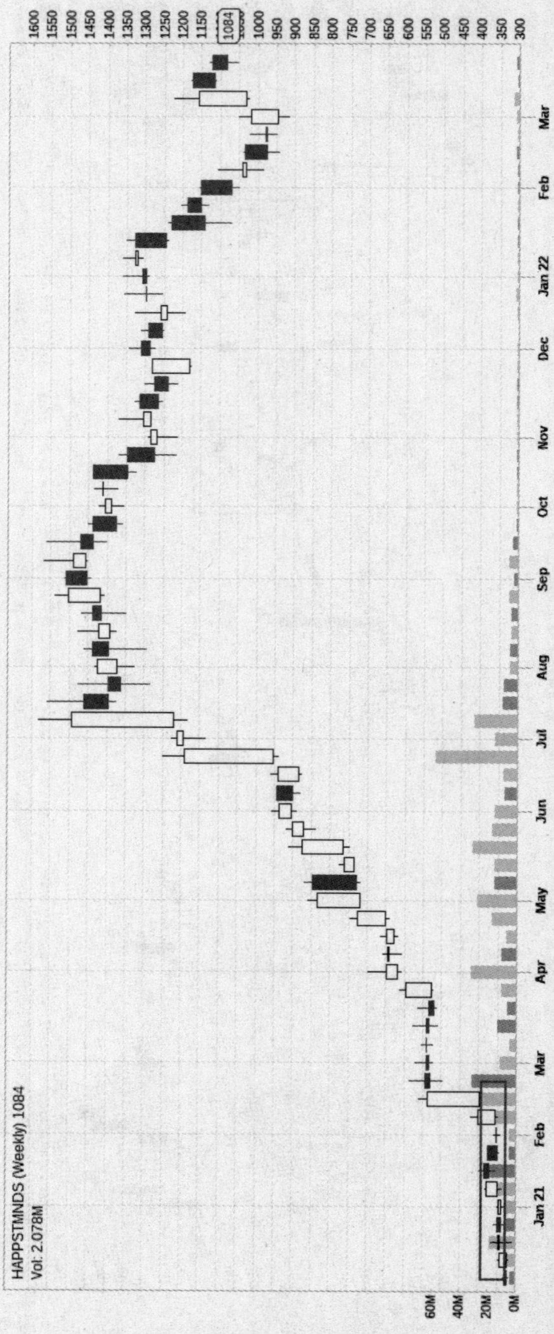
HAPPSTMNDS (Weekly) 1084
Vol: 2.078M

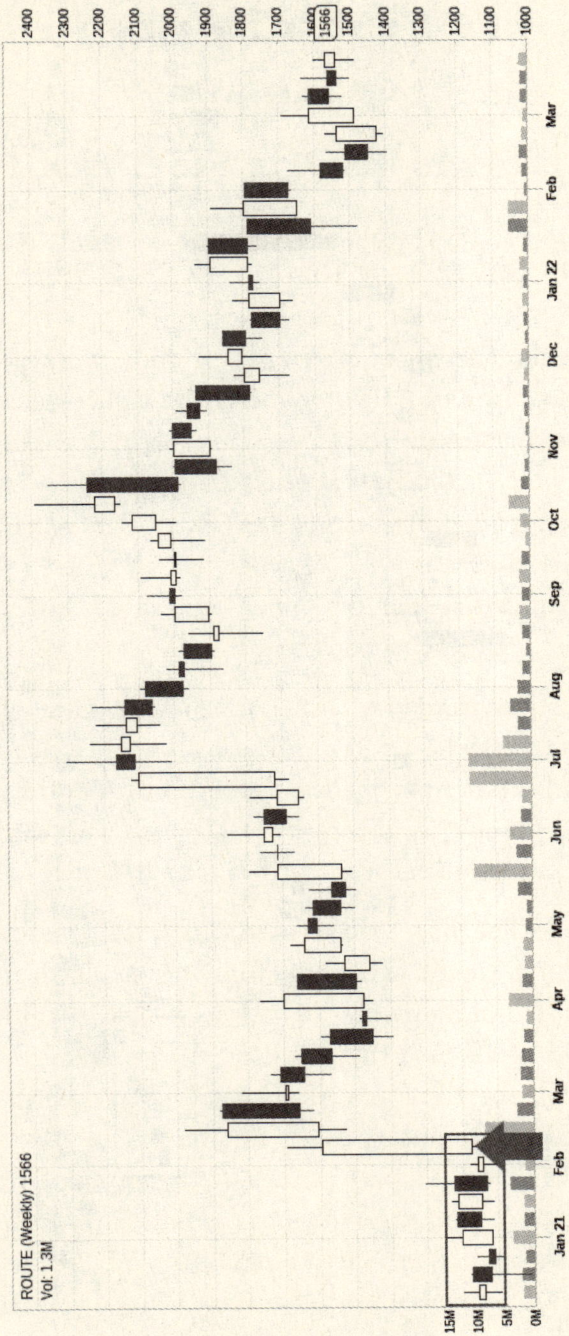
ROUTE (Weekly) 1566
Vol: 1.3M
2400
2300
2200
2100
2000
1900
1800
1700
1600
1566
1500
1400
1300
1200
1100
1000
15M
10M
5M
0M
Jan 21
Feb
Mar
Apr
May
Jun
Jul
Aug
Sep
Oct
Nov
Dec
Jan 22
Feb
Mar

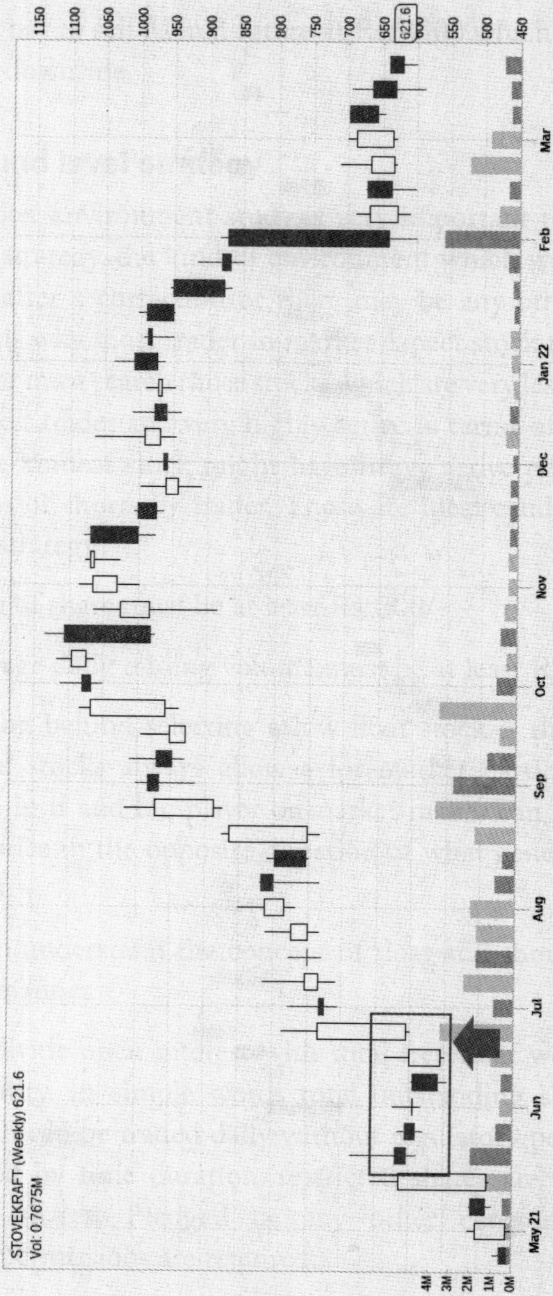
STOVEKRAFT (Weekly) 621.6
Vol: 0.7675M
May 21
Jun
Jul
Aug
Sep
Oct
Nov
Dec
Jan 22
Feb
Mar
1150
1100
1050
1000
950
900
850
800
750
700
650
621.6
550
500
450
4M
3M
2M
1M
0M

Strategy 5

2.5 Days Funda

There are several un-located and unheard trading strategies in the market. 2.5 days funda is one of those, I am sure this strategy is never heard before and it will be one of the most profitable one for you. As we have discussed earlier also that the market is always right and we as a trader are right only few times. Market and stocks will always behave the way they want even if the track is opposite to what it has been doing. Markets and stocks changes the trajectory suddenly and that is where the opportunity to implement 2.5 days ka funda is. It makes money when the stock's behavior reverses from its current trend and that is where we can earn.

The ground level strategy-

We need to understand that there are always short term trend changes and pull backs in the market and these trends gives us opportunities to earn good profits. While working on this particular strategy we will be trading a sudden fall in the price of the stock which has been into a quite great uptrend for a while. A sudden profit booking is faced by the stock and it starts falling. A lot of volume action is created by both retail as well as speculative trader. The one who keeps a close eye till 2.5 days is declared winner. We need to identify those stocks which are into a perfect uptrend and synchronized with the uptrend of the market, means the market must also be in an uptrend. Look for a fall with volume on the first day and fall with low volumes on the second day, on the third day in second half the stock tends to finish the profit taking and resumes its uptrend, it's a great time to make money.

How it works?

Let us understand why the overall change in the trend is there and why after 2.5 days the stock chases back the uptrend. A particular stock which has been in a great uptrend and has been making money for traders has to see profit booking someday, these swing position traders and especially speculative traders who have entered in the stock at lower level would like to book some profits and take money from the table, this particular activity gives a short term trend reversal to the stock which last for 2.5 days usually and some time for five days. You just need to assess it for 2.5 day or 5 days. If the stock, you are dealing is backed with good fundamentals and strong uptrend mostly it will be 2.5 days.

On first day of the fall the stock will fall in the first half with heavy volumes, and will keep grinding lower at this stage and intra-day trader who bought the stock burn their hands by the end of the day trade, either they have to cut the position or carry the trade to second day. Some of the retail investors also enter the stock with an attraction that a stock which was expensive has suddenly become cheap and will rebound by the day but at last their position are either to be sold or to be taken along next day. So basically the mindset is that a stock which was in clear uptrend and giving feeling on Fear of missing out (FOMO) to a lot of people suddenly falls due to profit booking and some retailers try to buy it first in the very first hour on day of fall and feel trapped by the end of the day.

On the second day the stock starts falling again, in general it will open around 2-3% lower but with lesser volume than the first day. The retail trader who have been holding the stock from yesterday will keep holding because his stop losses are not triggered yet by a small margin and hopping game starts. Some will even slowly start exiting their positions and will curse the market saying that a stock which was always in uptrend also starts falling as soon as he took this position.

Then comes the third day when the stock will again open in red zone but with thinner volume, now all the retail traders will lose patience and will have to sell the stock because the stop loss of stock is triggered. In the second half when the retail traders are done with their selling, Speculative traders enter the trade again and stock zooms with heavy volume.

Base mindset

For the lesser experience traders in the market it must be treated as a golden rule that 2.5 days ka funda is a strategy to use in an uptrend only, if you want to use the strategy in a downtrend or neutral market trend then gain some market experience first. Being a newbie use this strategy only when the market and the stock is in full uptrend.

Another very important point while adopting this strategy is that if the breakdown of the stock is happening on very low volumes than it does not fit in the strategy, it might be a false alarm and can end in two scenarios. Either a more painful fall with higher volumes will come or the stock will come back to its upwards trajectory on very next day. On both of the grounds it does not fit into 2.5 days strategy.

Look for the place to enter-

Most of the retail investors gets lured by the fall on day-1 and enter the stock as they see that the stock which was hitting roof is now down and think that it will recover at earliest. We must never enter into stock on day-1 and day 2. The best time enter is at first half on third day, That is why we say it 2.5 days when the selling pressure is almost done, selling volume are very thin and the stock is about to see a reversal in the temporary downtrend. It may happen that on third day general market like Sensex and Nifty opens gap up and stock may not open down but you should keep close watch in the first half and look for low risk entry point. Keep close watch on volume which should be lower in first half compare to previous two days.

The stoploss- yes it's the most important part! –

Keeping the stop loss of 2 to 3% is important or you may keep your stop loss just 1% below the low of three days.

Look at the quantity and risk capital

This strategy can give you big returns but it's a bit risky also, so always bet not more that .5% to 1% of your risk capital.

Exit at the right point

Targeting around 5 to 8% profit in these kinds of stock is not a bad idea at all as the stock and general market both are in quite uptrend the stock is meant to give strong returns when bought under 2.5 days ka funda.

What is it all about!

2.5 days ka funda is all about taking advantage of a contrarian move of the market. When the lake of returns in market is full, it would like to have some spillage and as a trader we have to take advantage of these spillages only. The most important point to note here is that the trader must not try to catch a falling knife which simply means that the trader must not try to buy on the first day when the fall is at initial level and on very large volume.

The first day sale of stock will continue for next 1.5 days as the speculative traders would like to take full advantage of the situation. Always look for a bounce back scenario and then wait for your profits to come. Another very important point to be noted here that you must choose those stocks only which are not part of any speculative trading and have great fundamentals & having nice bullish technical setup for better results.

Don't try to test your luck in bear market or a neutral market trend, it needs a lot of data and market indicators to do so in a falling market. Do it when you have got enough experience in the market and start understanding its movements.

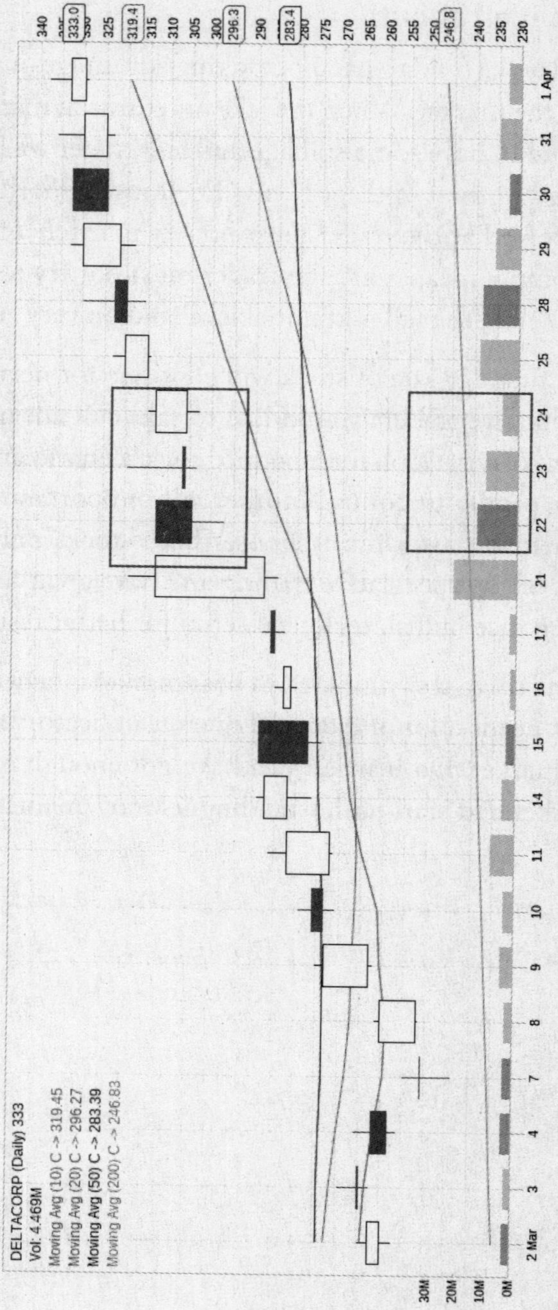
DELTACORP (Daily) 333
Vol: 4.469M
Moving Avg (10) C -> 319.45
Moving Avg (20) C -> 296.27
Moving Avg (50) C -> 283.39
Moving Avg (200) C -> 246.83

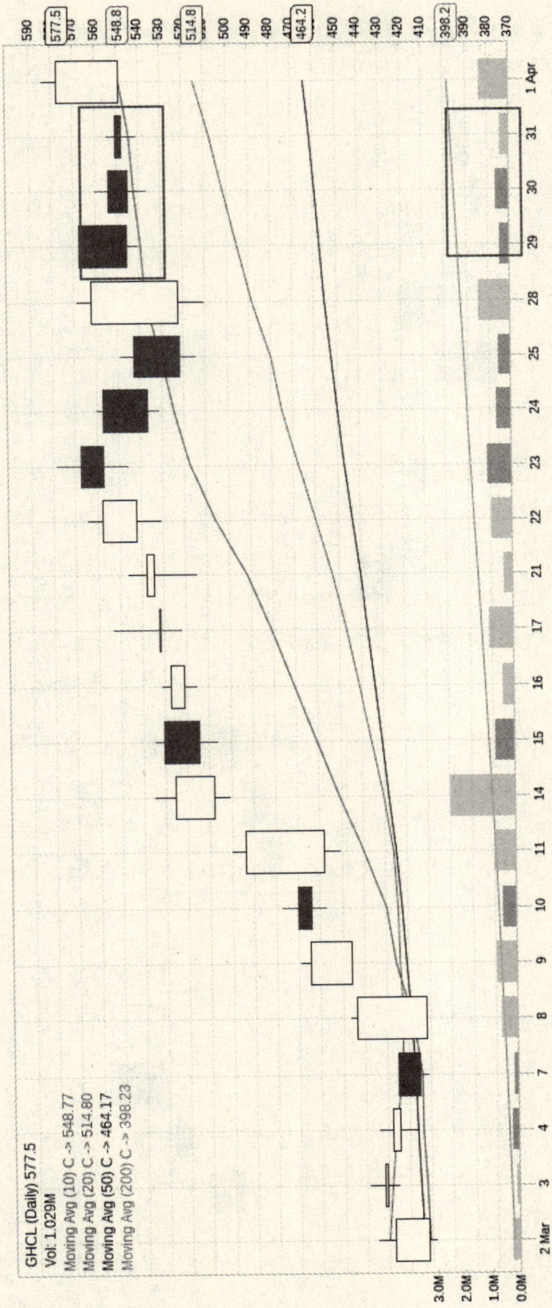
GHCL (Daily) 577.5
Vol: 1.029M
Moving Avg (10) C -> 548.77
Moving Avg (20) C -> 514.80
Moving Avg (50) C -> 464.17
Moving Avg (200) C -> 398.23

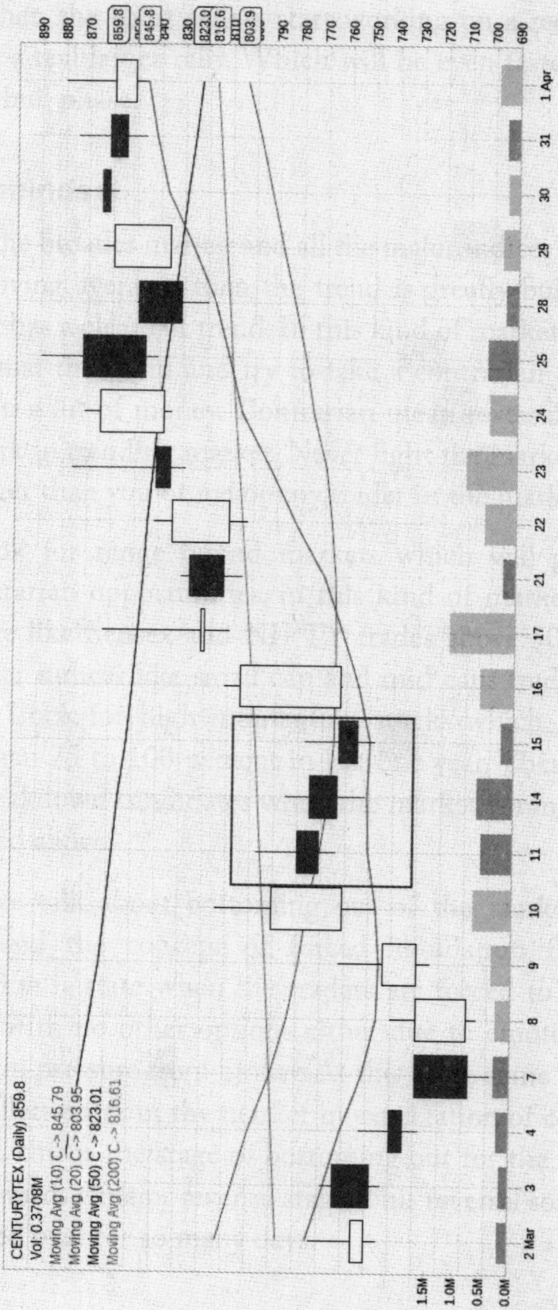
CENTURYTEX (Daily) 859.8
Vol: 0.3708M
Moving Avg (10) C -> 845.79
Moving Avg (20) C -> 803.95
Moving Avg (50) C -> 823.01
Moving Avg (200) C -> 816.61

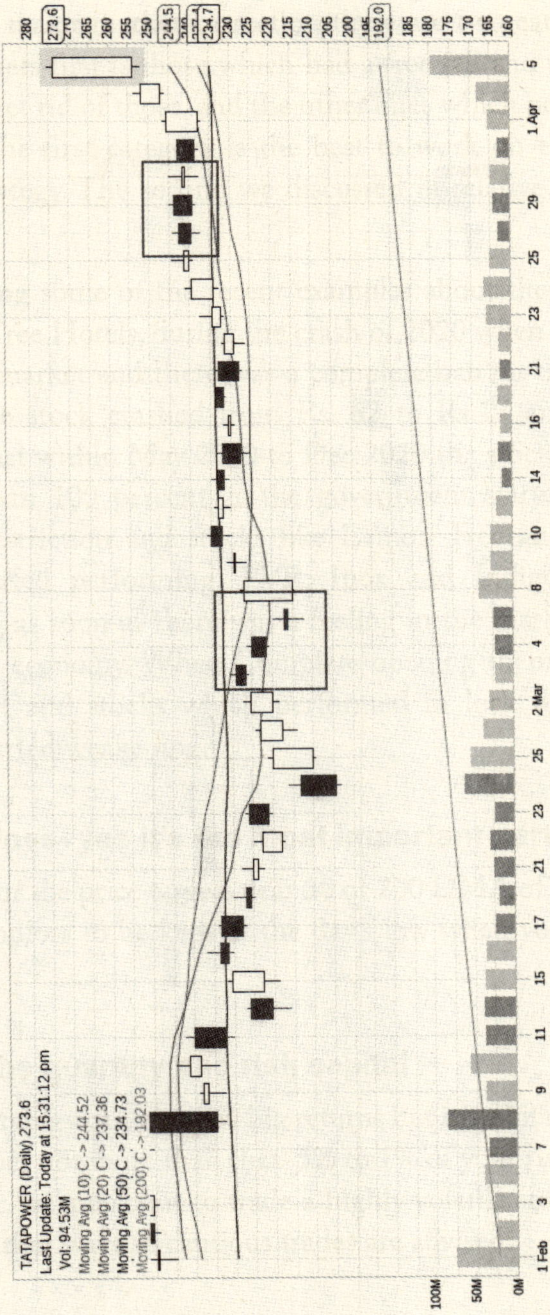
TATAPOWER (Daily) 273.6
Last Update: Today at 15:31:12 pm
Vol: 94.53M
Moving Avg (10) C -> 244.52
Moving Avg (20) C -> 237.36
Moving Avg (50) C -> 234.73
Moving Avg (200) C -> 192.03
1 Feb
3
7
9
11
15
17
21
23
25
2 Mar
4
8
10
14
16
21
23
25
29
1 Apr
5
100M
50M
0M
273.6
244.5
234.7
192.0

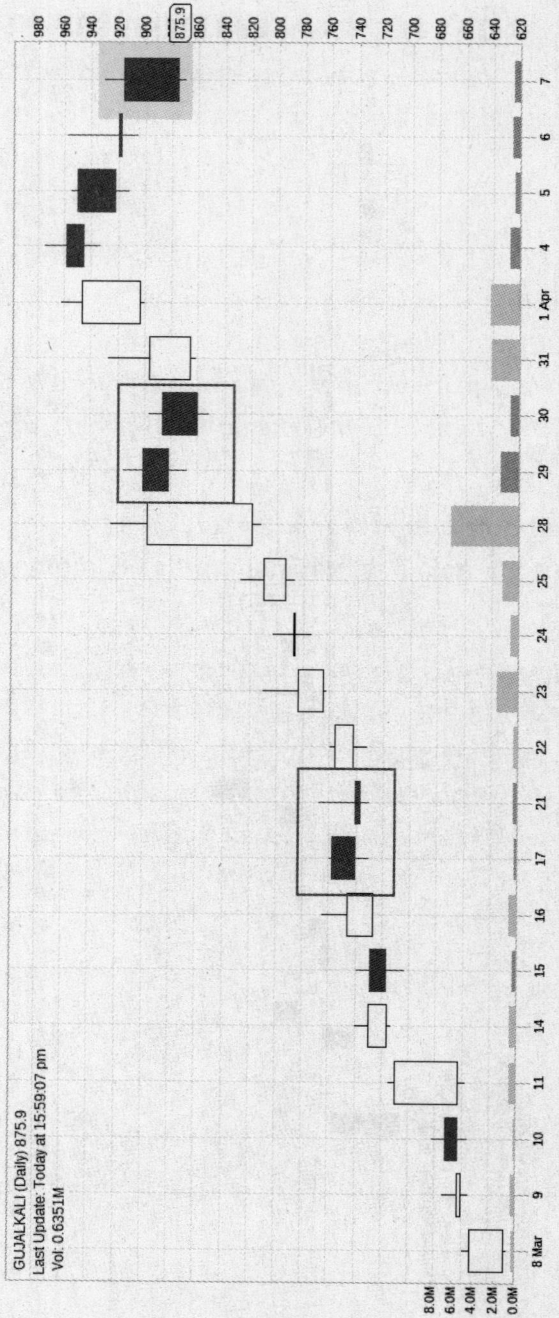
GUJALKALI (Daily) 875.9
Last Update: Today at 15:59:07 pm
Vol: 0.6351M
980
960
940
920
900
875.9
860
840
820
800
780
760
740
720
700
680
660
640
620
8.0M
6.0M
4.0M
2.0M
0.0M
8 Mar
9
10
11
14
15
16
17
21
22
23
24
25
28
29
30
31
1 Apr
4
5
6
7

STRATEGY 6

CROSSING THE PATH- WHERE MOVING AVERAGES CROSS EACH OTHER

In simple words a moving average crossover situation is that when a short term moving average crosses and closes above a long term moving average to form a bullish pattern. It's a vice-versa situation when a short term moving average crosses below the long term moving averages. It is formation of a bearish trend.

Swing Position traders can use moving averages of 10 days to 20 days to make gains on short term swing. Trend traders largely use long term moving average crossover like the 20 days EMA/50 days EMA or 50 days EMA /200 days EMA that are moreover signals of a long term trend.

The ground level strategy

For swing trading stocks, I have found the best crossover signals for trades that last a few days to weeks to be the following three:

1. 10 days EMA crosses 20 days EMA
2. 20 days EMA crosses 50 days EMA
3. 50 days EMA crosses 200 days EMA

Back Test

Buying on a crossover works too well when the data is back tested, we all know that moving averages are quantifiable and can be easily back tested. Back testing is simple testing of your sample size on some historical evidences. Any stock which comes under above mentioned crossovers must be added to your watch list and an analysis to be run with historical data. A trader just need to see the historical data and see how the stocks behaved when the same patterns were found on chart. Look for those ones which leaves some strong bullish signals. Largely the back testing for these crossovers can be done on a pre-decide stock list or on some major indices like NIFTY, Sensex or Bank NIFTY.

How it works

The back testing of data is very important step to identify the trade levels. Back testing of stocks' data will let a swing trader understand about the points where the stocks forms bullish pattern and swing trades can be profitable enough. Understand the range of bullish trend and take trade accordingly to make some gains. Also this is a strategy which can easily be back tested on a number of charts even by a beginner.

Base mindset

Exponential moving average crossover signals parameters:

1. Enter at the end of day based on short-term moving average crossing and closing over the long term moving average. It can be crossover of any of the above mentioned three types.

2. Second method to use moving average crossover signals is to find one that works well historically on average for a type of market.

   For example, 10-day/20 day EMA cross works as a profitable strategy on many recent IPOs to catch both swings and trends trading in price.

The simplest principle for moving average crossover signals that create profitability is that if historical evidences are there telling you that capturing a move at that price point will give you better profits. Also if the stock's short term crosses below a long term then it's a sign of exiting the stock and keep your losses at minimum.

Look for the place to enter

Check the price level which are "more profitable", sometime getting late will not give you great levels. Sometime the trader buys the stock on the upper side of upswing then he finds that sizable amount of profit is already lost. At this point the share is a bit overbought and the risk/reward ratio is not that profitable to get into trade.

The stop loss- yes it's the most important part!

1. Set a stop loss when the shorter- term moving average crossing under the longer term moving average. Like if

the 10 days moving average crossing under 20 day moving average.

2. Keeping a trailing stop loss allows a profitable trade continue until the shorter-term moving average crossing under the longer term moving average.

3. You can also use a trailing stop of a close below the previous day's low or a large bearish reversal candle for a tight trade.

Look at the quantity and risk capital

More than 1% of capital should not be risked on crossover trades.

Exit at the right point

To check for an exit point, a swing trader can use either back testing technique or can do it mechanically. If the back testing gives you the data that average profitable trade was for around 12% gains then it becomes an exit point for you. This simply means that a trader should book profits when the stock is trading above 10% from the entry point. On the other hand, a mechanical swing trader can create a system using the best signal for each charts on their watch list and just take the entry and exist, letting the system play out as profitable by catching the big wins by risking open profits.

What is it all about!

Trading on crossovers can work as a mechanical or discretionary signal. There are traders which follow the crossover religiously and take positions accordingly. For these traders entry and exit point are preset. On the other hand, there are traders who are mechanical swing traders who are seasoned trader and don't want to introduce emotions or regret into their strategy. For these traders the theory is that there are no right or wrong way to trade, it largely depends on how they want to trade.

Moving averages are a great direction for a swing trader, bigger gains than losses on average are made when the trader has a process to do so. So, keep looking for charts well and identify the crossovers and profitable points to make money. I would like to say that moving average crossover is simplest, most commonly used yet very effective swing trading strategy. That is why Golden crossover and Death crossover are being tracked and used even by many fundamental investors.

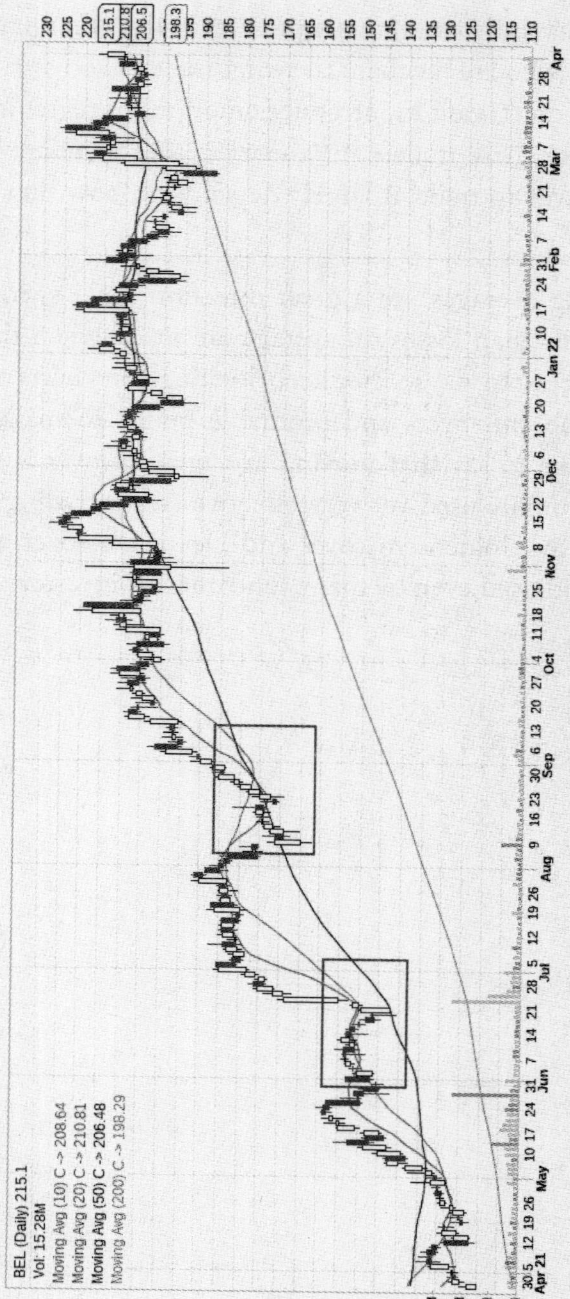
BEL (Daily) 215.1
Vol: 15.28M
Moving Avg (10) C -> 208.64
Moving Avg (20) C -> 210.81
Moving Avg (50) C -> 206.48
Moving Avg (200) C -> 198.29

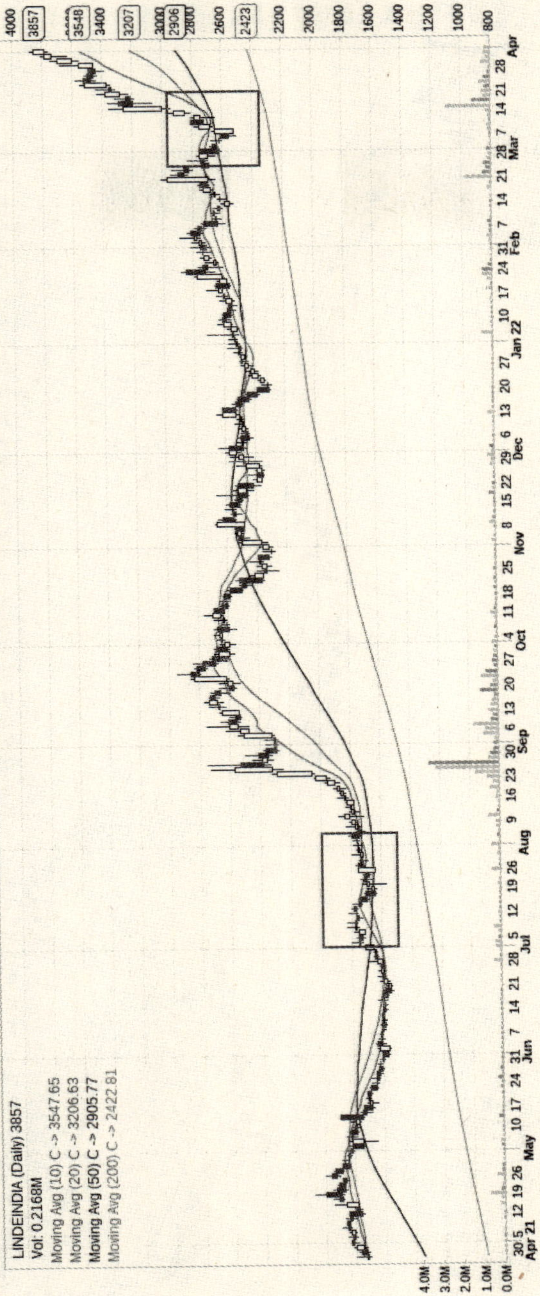
LINDEINDIA (Daily) 3857
Vol: 0.2168M
Moving Avg (10) C -> 3547.65
Moving Avg (20) C -> 3206.63
Moving Avg (50) C -> 2905.77
Moving Avg (200) C -> 2422.81

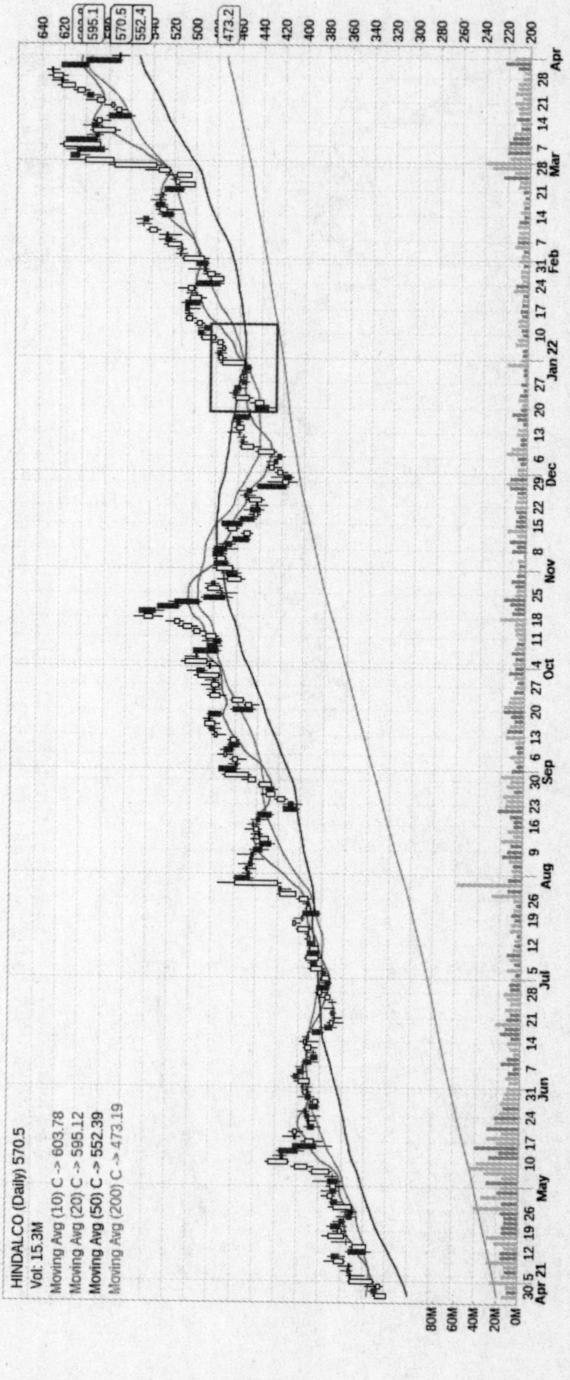
HINDALCO (Daily) 570.5
Vol: 15.3M
Moving Avg (10) C -> 603.78
Moving Avg (20) C -> 595.12
Moving Avg (50) C -> 552.39
Moving Avg (200) C -> 473.19

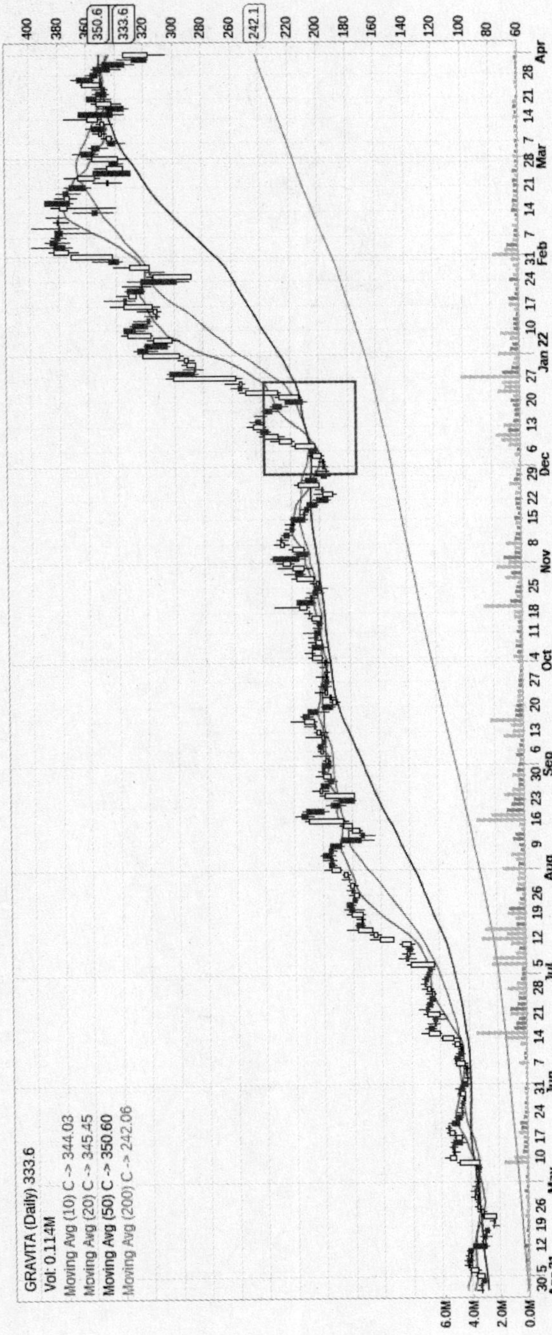
GRAVITA (Daily) 333.6
Vol: 0.114M
Moving Avg (10) C -> 344.03
Moving Avg (20) C -> 345.45
Moving Avg (50) C -> 350.60
Moving Avg (200) C -> 242.06
350.6
333.6
242.1

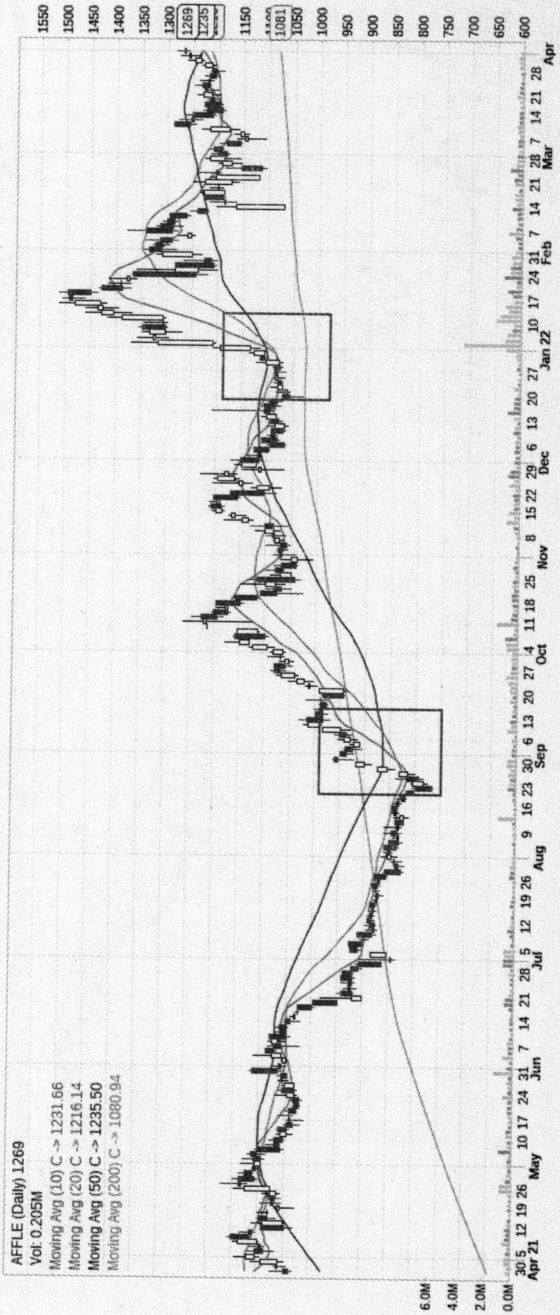
AFFLE (Daily) 1269
Vol: 0.205M
Moving Avg (10) C -> 1231.66
Moving Avg (20) C -> 1216.14
Moving Avg (50) C -> 1235.50
Moving Avg (200) C -> 1080.94

STRATEGY 7

PERFORMANCE MATTERS

Sailing in the boat of quarterly results the stock market works on various piece of news and what can be a larger news than stock's earning itself? In a year every listed company has to declare the earnings four time i.e. every quarter. In this announcement the company tells the shareholder and general public about how much it sold and earned in the preceding quarter. As soon as the earnings are declared it becomes a news for the stock and traders become active to trade.

Earnings of a stock are so important for a stock that it can even change the trend of a stock, sometime the entire industry. Few years back when Infosys used to be the first company to report its earning in NIFTY, it used to decide about how the entire IT pack would behave for next few days.

Post Earning Announcement Drift (P.E.A.D.) is such an important strategy to trade in market that can make some real strong money for a trader. The basic theory behind this strategy is that every stock shows a gap-up on better-than-expected earnings and the trend may continue for several weeks. The better impact of P.E.A.D strategy can be seen in intra-day trades during very next day of the result declarations, in swing trades for around a week and while taking swing trade you may look for around 3 weeks to 10 weeks.

The ground level strategy

Always keep a close eye in the earning announcement timeline. It can happen either during the market hours or after that. In these announcements what we look for on the long side is:

1. The stock which has gained more than 3-5% on more than three times its 50-day average daily traded volume.
2. The volume should be at least 50% higher than previous day
3. Trading above its 50-day price moving average
4. Price of the stock must be more than Rs. 300/-

Average daily traded volume must be more than Rs.1 Cr.

How it works

There might be several reasons for stocks drifting in the direction of the initial market reaction

1. During the initial days of a new information which is result declaration, traders and investors tend to under react or unable to understand the results. After few days you will observe an opposite reaction. At this point they start thinking that they missed an opportunity by not reacting at the time and then they come to the market with an overreaction.
2. Institutions and HNI don't buy instantly, they research for few days and when they understand real growth of the company then they take new positions.

3. When Institutions buy in a big way, Short sellers tend to cover at higher prices, even short sellers add fuel to fire due by short covering.

On the other side if the stock reports worse than expected earning then the stock keep drifting lower for many days or weeks, because it takes time for a trend to capture the stock. Under this strategy stock market reacting to the earnings is the major theme. Remember, it's not about the earning itself rather market's reaction over its earning is a key factor. Market are always forward looking and if the company reports a strong earnings for the quarter or shows signals of strong upcoming quarters then market shall always react to that.

Positive and negative earning both allows a stock to react because of FOMO. It creates a Fear of Missing Out in the market, when the stock presents good earning then traders don't want to lose owning the next big winner and on other side when earnings are missed the traders sheds the position at earliest as it does not want to lose further.

During the COVID wave and partial recovery, Reliance Retail was the market hero and kept on hitting sixes quarter on quarter. The overall RIL thing shifted to its performance, which was few years back dependent on Oil to Chemical segment. Reacting on results is outcome of market perception also, for example if Infosys declares 10% growth then the market may not react much on the other hand if Paytm just reduces losses, the market may give it a thumbs up.

Base mindset

This trading strategy works beautifully when the markets are in a downturn or a bearish phase. At this time everyone wants to sell and nobody is expecting greater surprises out of the stocks. Companies which performs better are rewarded by the market always. A lot of Indian banks were performing well after the meltdown of 2008. They all were making profits where global peers were going bankrupt. Big surprise is that in market when there is very low expectation from the market and certain stocks come up with great earnings. In the recent time after COVID melt down Chemical stocks performed well quarter on quarter. Same way during Russia and Ukraine war commodity got expensive and same resulted in financials of commodity companies like Tata steel and Hindalco and they performed well quarter on quarter as positive surprise was there on street.

A trader must always remember that like other strategies this also generate few false alarms as not every time the market reacts positive on earnings. Sometime the market is so pessimistic that it ignores every positive sign. Just then the game begins. Surprisingly, when people ignore and forget all about it, it begins to work again.

Look for the place to enter

1. You can buy at the same time when the earnings are out, check for a small base above a stock's Volume Weighted Moving Average Price to take some long strategies. Also, buying the intraday breakout is good.

2. Buying in the next day of earning is also good if we get levels of earlier day's high.

3. When the stock is in sideways consolidation above a rising 10 or 20 day EMA. Once the breakout is there, it will be a right point to buy.

The stop loss- yes it's the most important part!

The stoploss is half a percent below the lows of the entry day or right below a stock's 10/20 day EMA.

Look at the quantity and risk capital

Risk 1% of capital during market uptrends - when all major market stock indices large and small cap tend to trade above their 50-day moving averages. Risk 0.5% of capital during range-bound markets when some of the major indices are below 50-day EMA and some are above.

Exit at the right point

There is something very good about this strategy, as the reaction on the earnings sustains for a longer period of time it gives opportunity to all three type of traders namely Intraday, Swing and Position. Following are certain exit scenarios:

1. Exit within 2.5 to 8 trading days when taken a swing trades and 2.5 to 8 weeks when buy is taken as a position trade.

2. In case of swing trade you may, sell half 2.5 to 5 days after the buy. Sell the pending quantity on a close below a stock's 10/20 day EMA.

3. In terms of position trade, the trader must sell 50% of position after 2.5 up weeks in a row. Sell the rest 50% on a close below a stock's 50-day simple moving average.

What is it all about!

Earnings reports are always a key point for a stock's performance. An earnings report can allow the stock to react either ways, it can either start a fresh long term trend or end an existing one. Sometime trader forgets the rule of trading under this strategy. Rather than paying attention to the market's reaction on the stock they start analysing the stock's earning, which is not the right thing to do. Remember, we must always pay attention on the trend of the market after earning declaration by the company. If you see a strong momentum stock declining even after better than expected earnings performance, then it's a clear sign of uptrend getting over for the stock. Always focus on market reaction and not your opinion about the results.

On the other hand,

Only earnings will not give a great trend to the stock, it must be supported with the following conditions:

Good market reaction post earning–Only good results are not enough, market participants must buy the good news that is more important. Lot of time the market does not respond well to great earnings and on the other hand some of the average earners are lauded heavily. It is all about the game of expectations of market participants.

Powerful earnings and sales acceleration–The legacy and outperformance related to that is also very important. Many time we see stocks which have been very conservative in terms of earning and suddenly give a spike in number. Just imagine TCS's earning growing by 30% in dollar terms in any quarter, the stock will hit the roof.

Earning surprise in a non-favourite stock – Think about a very conservative and non-favourite stock which comes with a sudden surprise. For example, Government owned oil companies which are never market favourite because of lot of government intervention. If BPCL gives an earnings growth of 50% in a particular quarter then trader will not buy it immediately.

A comparative smaller cap for the company and a lesser float in market will always give larger wings to a stock when there is an earning surprise. Sometime the earning gap strategy can be a perfect long term position trade to be taken in. The stock keeps surprising the market with consecutive earnings but remember when the price starts reflecting in market expectation means the price reaches to that level that it has become habitual of best in class earning. A negative quarter can put a full stop on the trend.

A good earnings trend attracts everyone in the market whether a smaller investor, HNI or even Institutional investors and if the money is coming from the large ones, it allows stronger retail participation also to make money.

Example 1 – BSE – Stock has delivered superb results in last 4 quarters and every time near and after results stock moves. Also stock has given more than 4x returns in last 4 quarters. In swing every time in last 4 quarters there was opportunity.

Date(Transcript)	EPS	%Chg	Sales(Cr)	%Chg
Dec-21	4.42	+96%	213.1	+35%
Sep-21	4.69	+41%	219.3	+46%
Jun-21	3.74	+60%	179.8	+14%
Mar-21	2.29	+469%	165.3	+10%

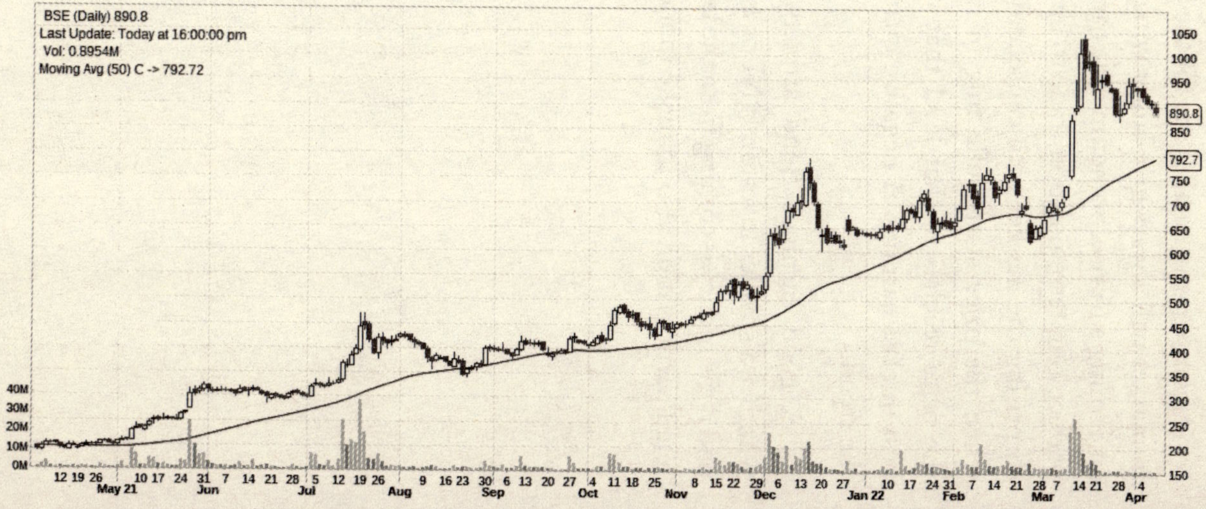

Example 2 – Gravita– Stock has delivered superb results in last 3 quarters and every time near and after results stock moves. Also stock has 3x in last 3 quarters. Everytime near results in last 3 quarters there was opportunity for swing trading.

Date(Transcript)	EPS	%Chg	Sales(Cr)	%Chg
Dec-21	5.81	+149%	556.6	+49%
Sep-21	5.46	+227%	546.5	+61%
Jun-21	3.22	+465%	446.4	+73%

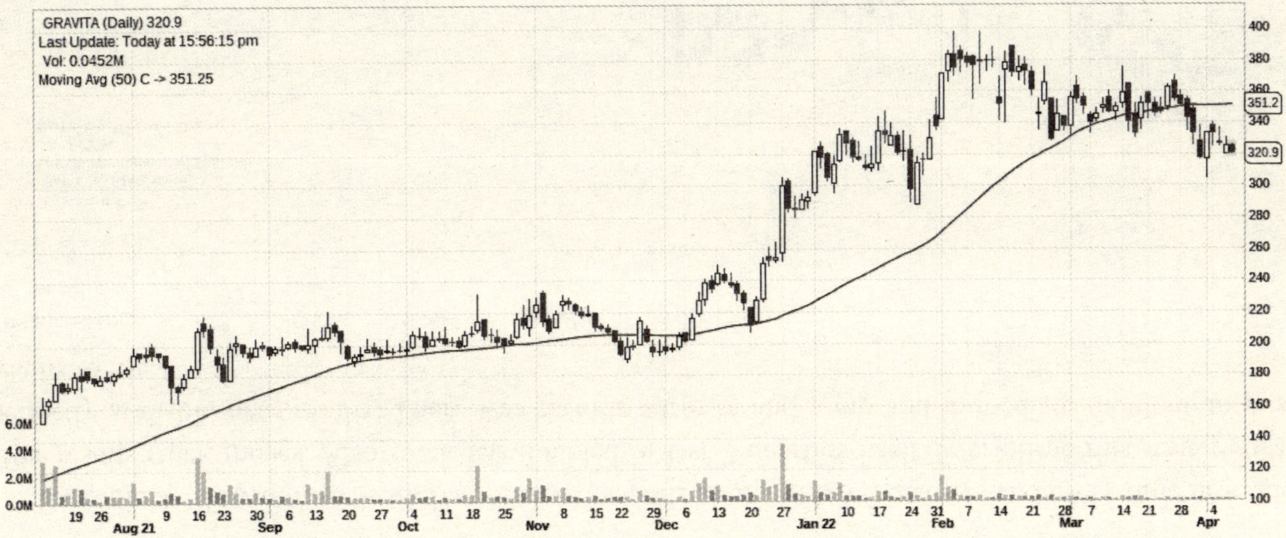

Example 3 – Raymond– Stock has delivered superb results in last 2 quarters and every time near and after results stock moves. Also stock has doubled in last 2 quarters itself. Every time this strategy was perfectly available near results. There was earning surprise and jump and immediate momentum post results to use.

Date(Transcript)	EPS	%Chg	Sales(Cr)	%Chg
Dec-21	15.06	+362%	1,843.4	+48%
Sep-21	8.00	+140%	1,551.3	+130%

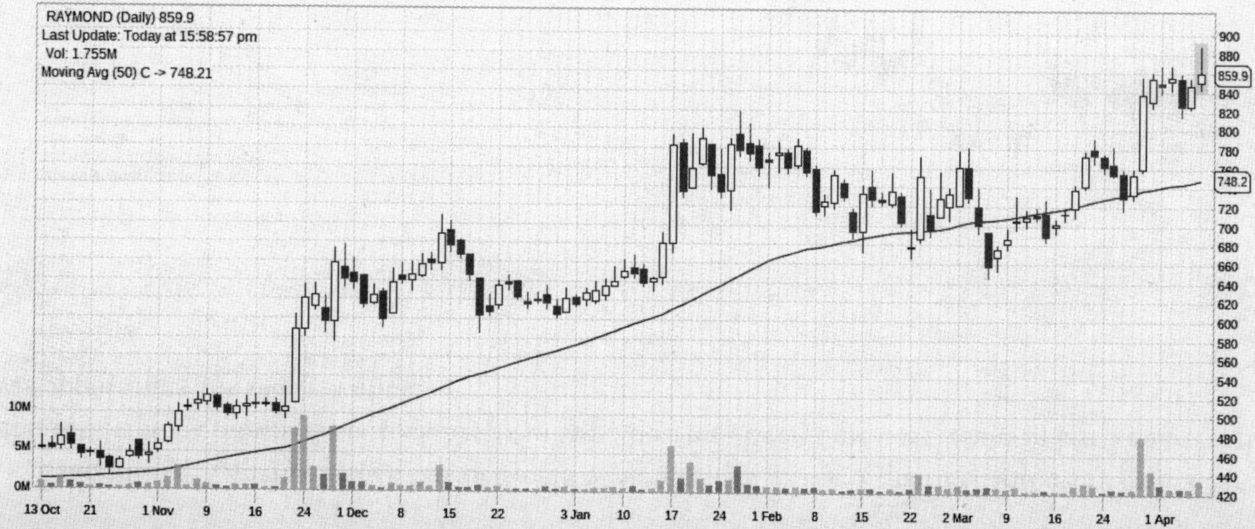

Example 4 – GNFC– Stock delivered better than expected December 2021 results and stock blasted post that.

Date(Transcript)	EPS	%Chg	Sales(Cr)	%Chg
Dec-21	34.79	+123%	2,380.3	+58%
Sep-21	18.31	+102%	2,095.9	+77%
Jun-21	15.56	+8089%	1,394.3	+99%

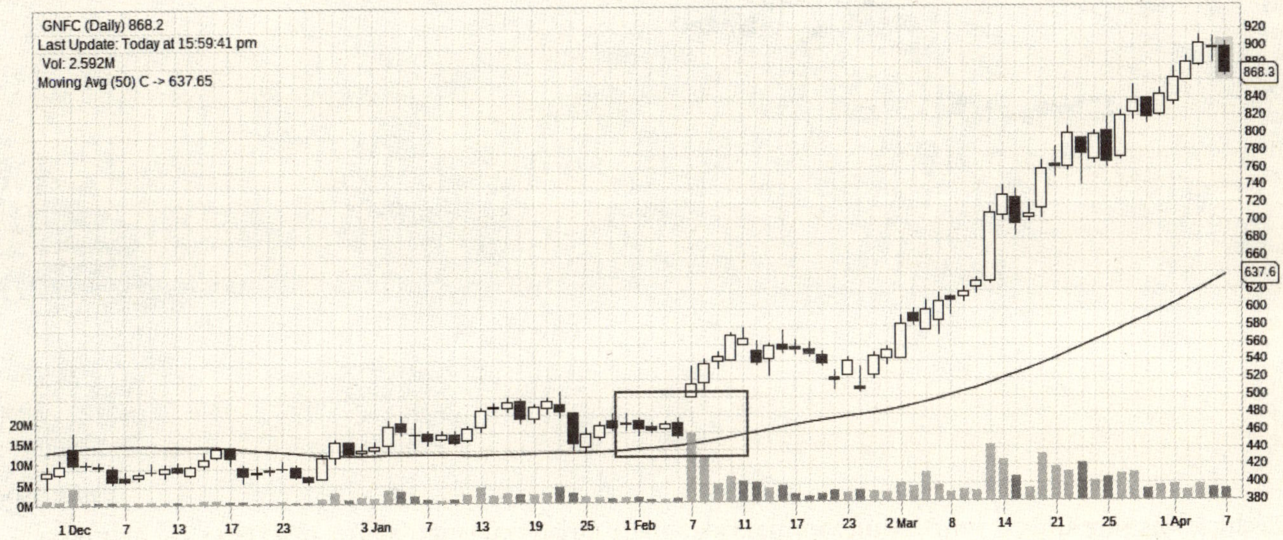

Example 5 – GMDC– Stock delivered better than expected December 2021 results and stock blasted post that.

Date(Transcript)	EPS	%Chg	Sales(Cr)	%Chg
Dec-21	4.71	+5333%	724.6	+102%
Sep-21	1.27	+234%	451.9	+92%

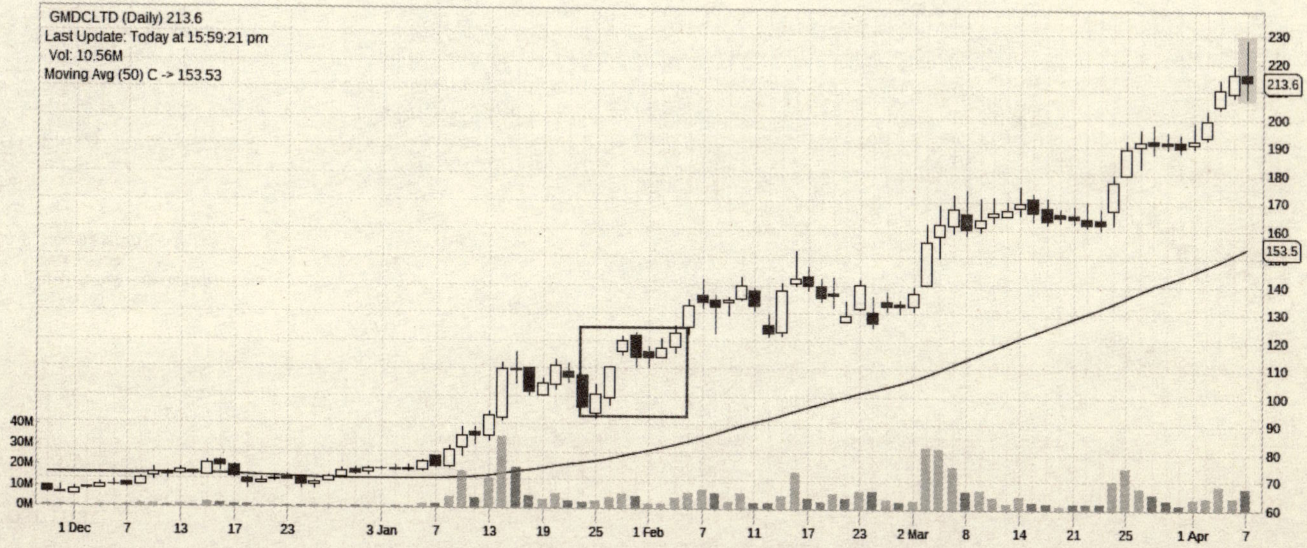

Example 6 – Sharda Cropchem– Stock delivered better than expected December 2021 results and stock blasted post that. Results was better than expected that is why it blasted since then.

Date(Transcript)	EPS	%Chg	Sales(Cr)	%Chg
Dec-21	11.33	+112%	879.8	+78%
Sep-21	3.55	+68%	642.8	+51%
Jun-21	4.22	+37%	622.7	+60%

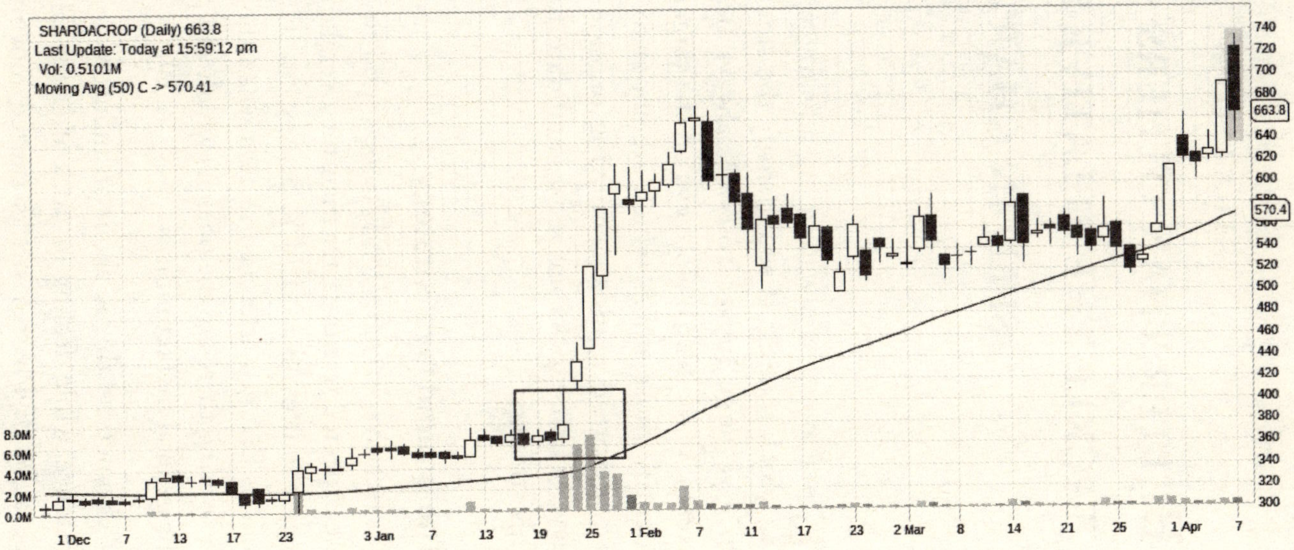

STRATEGY 8

BETTER THAN OTHERS – HOW TO TACKLE THE RELATIVE STRENGTH SEEN IN CHARTS

First mover is always a big advantage, even if you are in stock trading. If you identify the stocks which are about to give large moves you will always be able to skim the cream. If we keep a close eye on the targeted market, we can identify those stocks which are about to give a breakout in a widespread market or moving on side-lines for so many days. These stocks are ideal candidate to be bought under this strategy.

The ground level strategy

Relative strength tends to be found in those stocks which are expected to run faster than the overall market specially the major indices like NIFTY, Sensex etc. This relative strength tells us that just after a correction when the overall markets are recovering there are the pockets which will perform better than the general market indices.

Sometime this is about an industry or a single stock. For instance, while dealing in stock after the fall of 2020 we could see a lot of Pharma stocks started moving, reason was very obvious that the whole world was fighting with a pandemic and Pharma had to play a front role & was considered as safe haven for investments. Even IT and ITES stocks recovered faster than the overall market, the reason was simple, during COVID lockdowns the requirement of internet and tech based products shot up and everyone started looking for a value buy as well as growth buy in this industry.

In first quarter of 2022 Nifty made its bottom on 8 March at 15700 while GNFC made its bottom on 24 February at 505 by the time nifty made its bottom on 8 March it was trading above 605 which was 20% above from its bottom it was clear sign of relative strength of GNFC and early leadership. By 5 April GNFC was trading around 900. This is an example how much money can be made by being vigilant. If you listen to the market you are going to be rewarded. GNFC was clear cut example of abnormal strength in a weak market. Same happened in GHCL and GMDC in March 2022.

How to find relative strength:

Keep looking for following factors

1. Have a track of those stocks which have significantly gained in terms of pricing for last month, 3 months to 6 months, this price range can be from 10 to 50%.

2. Stock must be in price range of Minimum Rs. 300.

3. Average daily turnover must be more than 1 crore.

4. A trader can buy on a breakout to new 50-day highs or after bigger than 3 to 5% bounce with volume from a rising 10 or 20 day EMA.

How it works

One important thing which relative strength shows us about the institutional buyers, it tells us if the big ones are accumulating or distributing the stocks or an Industry, which ultimately decides the price targets of the stock. It's important to look for the big players' activities because they are the one who impact the market in every sense, either in terms of volume, price or trend of a stock or in industry. When the big funds are doing an activity in the market they are not looking for some intraday gains rather their target is to accumulate for long term.

We should always take of relative strength in comparative sense, in a roaring bull market when almost every stock is gaining 10 to 25% in that case if some stock gives 100% returns in same time period then there is a strong reason to buy it. Only big funds or an ultra-confident buyer can buy a stock at levels like 52 week or all-time high.

I remember between the rally of 2003 to 2007 the investors were running behind the telecom sector as it was the theme to get into, Bharti Airtel being the largest player always used to command most premium valuation and by the time it never went for lesser P/E multiple. The reason was simple whenever it went down there was an intuitional buyer ready to accumulate it. That is why we must keep looking for Large Players' activity zone to trace where the relative strength is.

Base mindset

Strategy to trade relative strength works in all type of market trends whether it is in bullish trend, consolidation or a further breakout after a consolidation. In a confirmed uptrend of the market, a trader must look at the stocks which are having highest momentum, these are for sure winning candidates. While the market is in a consolidation mode, a trader must look for stocks which are consolidating. These stocks can give huge breakout trade when the market starts rebounding after bottoming out.

Look for the place to enter

Always look for a breakout near 50 day moving average or after a long term consolidation. As soon as the market will start recovering, these breakout stocks will be the best ones to perform in coming days. Look for a recovery after a correction of 10% or above in NIFTY. If a trader can identify breakout candidates during that time period, it will be the best stock for both swing trade as well as positional trade.

The stoploss- yes it's the most important part!

The stop loss at half a percent below the lows of your entry day or at the current 10/20 or 50 day EMA.

Look at the quantity and risk capital

For a swing trade a trader must not risk more than 1% for its overall risk capital, for example if you buy Power Grid on Rs. 120 and your stop loss is at Rs. 8 below the buying price. Your total risk comes out to be 7000 as 1% of 7 lacs of your risk capital, the number of shares you can buy is 875.

Exit at the right point

Before entering into a trade a trader must always do the homework for the holding time frame of the stock. A swing trader trades to look for multiple opportunities to gain 5 to 20% rather than sitting in a stock for medium to very-very long term. This is the reason why selling after 2.5 to 5 day upward movement is a good thing to do or a trader can look for a close below a 10/20 or 50 day EMA (exponential moving average) as trailing stop loss.

What is it all about!

Always look for a pullback within a Bull Market it will give you a lot of trading ideas. The stocks which are still trading or holding above 50 day moving averages are our target stock always. You will find a lot of high growth names in market which will give a free fall during a correction within a roaring bull market. Remember, these are the stocks which will fantastically outperform when there is a sharp recovery. Unlike other defensives like FMCG which will do good when the market falls but do nothing when the market recovers. In a growing market you will never find any relative strength in defensives, they will only have this feature in a bear market or in a bull market correction.

That is why I say do not buy supposed good stock in the market on the way down rather look for better than others using relative strength. The big money makers generally have high relative strength.

A very deep correction which might finally turn into a short term bear market may range between 25 to 30% in major indices like NIFTY and Sensex. You will find many stocks which will fall 70 to 80% in the market. It does happen because they have high momentum but also remember during recovery in coming time period, these are the candidates which will recover very fast when the trend reverses. How to play this type of stocks we discussed in other chapter in the name of mean reversal.

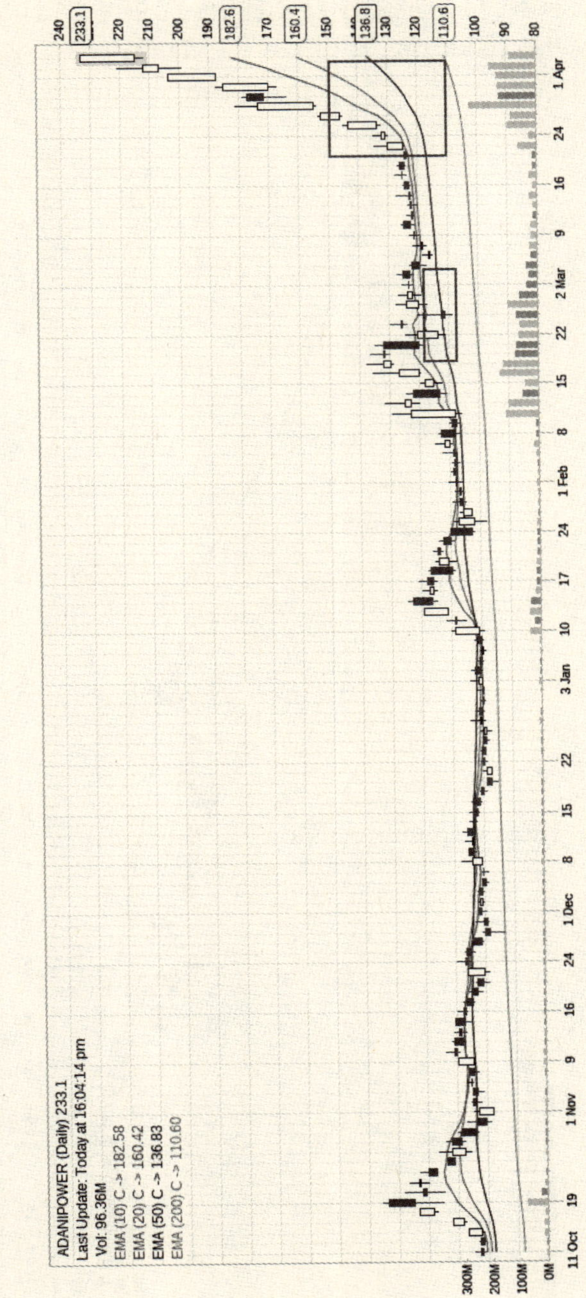
ADANIPOWER (Daily) 233.1
Last Update: Today at 16:04:14 pm
Vol: 96.36M
EMA (10) C -> 182.58
EMA (20) C -> 160.42
EMA (50) C -> 136.83
EMA (200) C -> 110.60

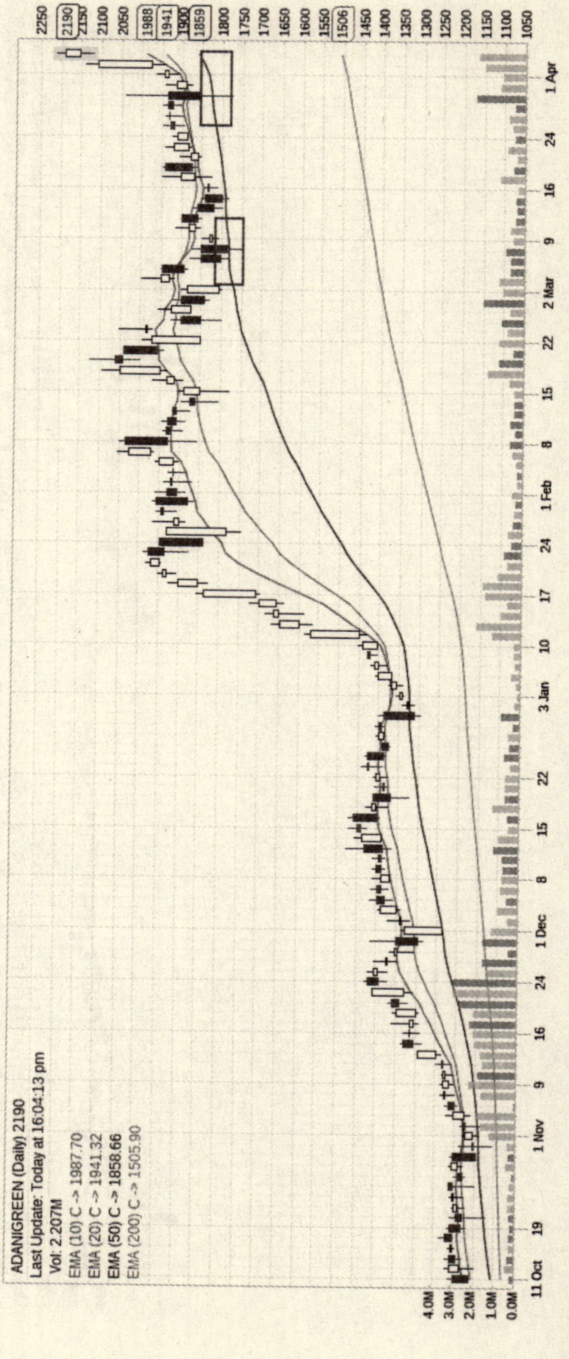
ADANIGREEN (Daily) 2190
Last Update: Today at 16:04:13 pm
Vol: 2.207M
EMA (10) C -> 1987.70
EMA (20) C -> 1941.32
EMA (50) C -> 1858.66
EMA (200) C -> 1505.90

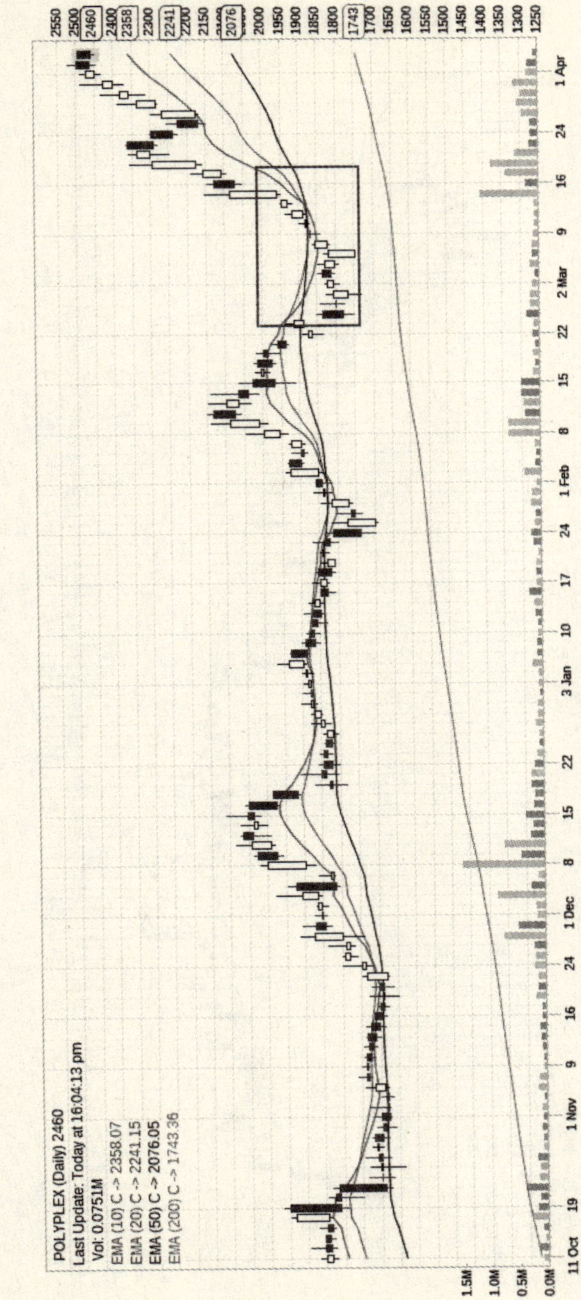
POLYPLEX (Daily) 2460
Last Update: Today at 16:04:13 pm
Vol: 0.0751M
EMA (10) C -> 2358.07
EMA (20) C -> 2241.15
EMA (50) C -> 2076.05
EMA (200) C -> 1743.36

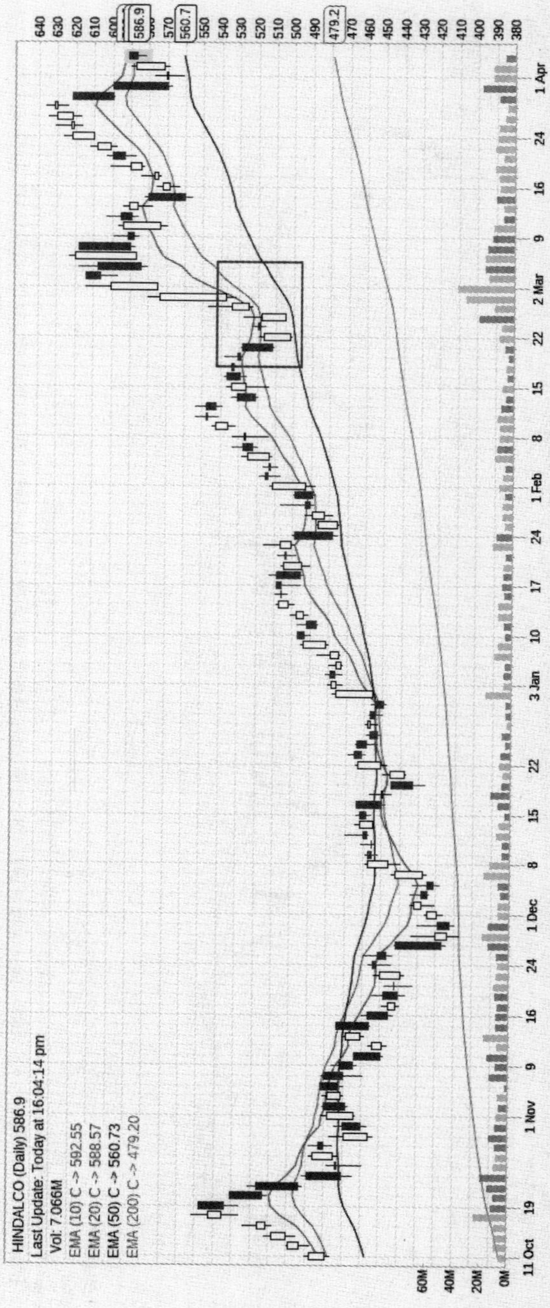
HINDALCO (Daily) 586.9
Last Update: Today at 16:04:14 pm
Vol: 7.066M
EMA (10) C -> 592.55
EMA (20) C -> 588.57
EMA (50) C -> 560.73
EMA (200) C -> 479.20
586.9
560.7
479.2
640
630
620
610
570
550
540
530
520
510
500
490
470
460
450
440
430
420
410
400
390
380
60M
40M
20M
0M
11 Oct
19
1 Nov
9
16
24
1 Dec
8
15
22
3 Jan
10
17
24
1 Feb
8
15
22
2 Mar
9
16
24
1 Apr

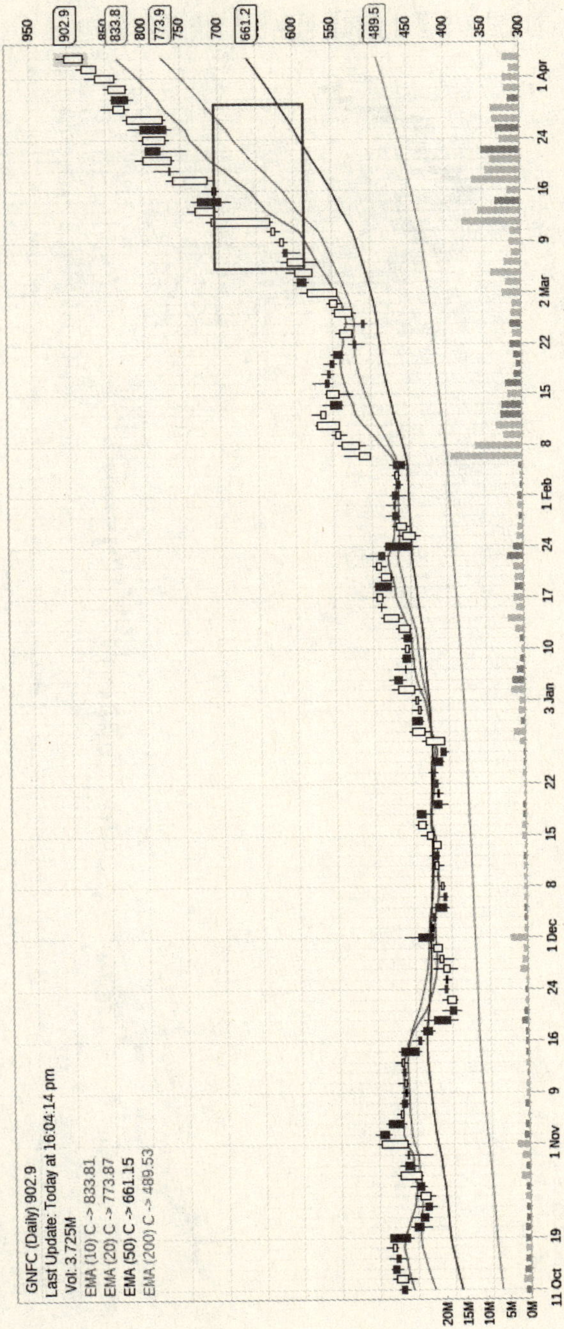
GNFC (Daily) 902.9
Last Update: Today at 16:04:14 pm
Vol: 3.725M
EMA (10) C -> 833.81
EMA (20) C -> 773.87
EMA (50) C -> 661.15
EMA (200) C -> 489.53

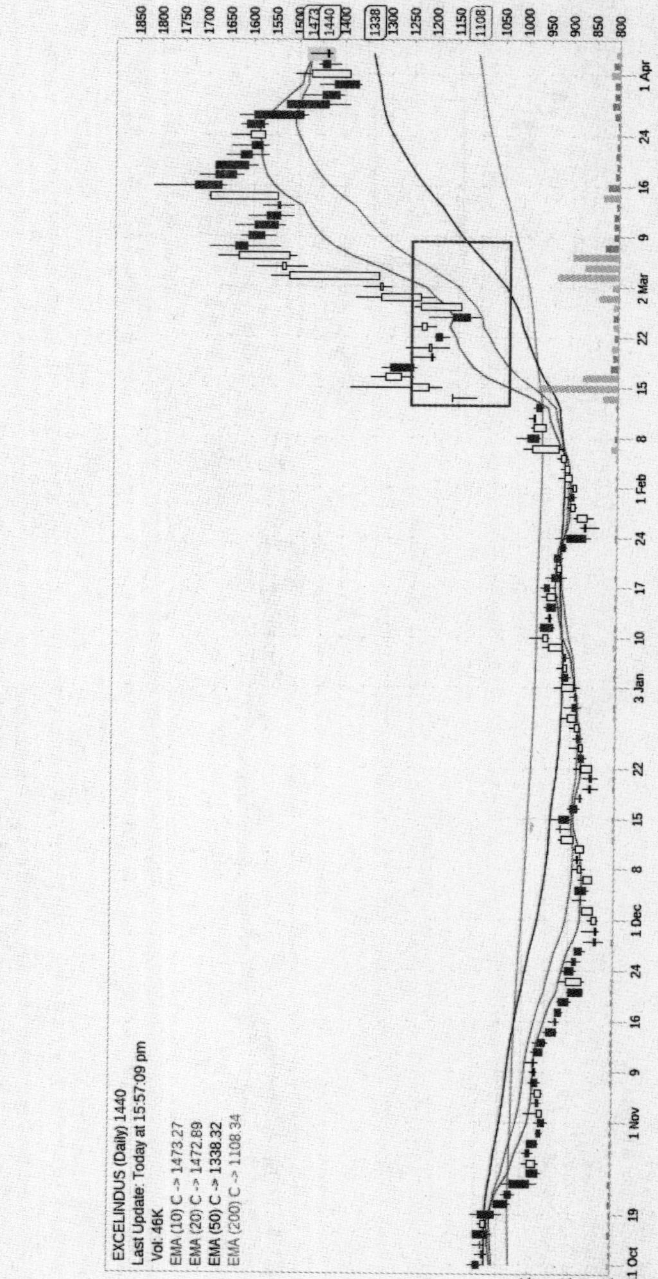

EXCELINDUS (Daily) 1440
Last Update: Today at 15:57:09 pm
Vol: 46K
EMA (10) C -> 1473.27
EMA (20) C -> 1472.89
EMA (50) C -> 1338.32
EMA (200) C -> 1108.34
1850
1800
1750
1700
1650
1600
1550
1500
1473
1440
1400
1338
1300
1250
1200
1150
1108
1050
1000
950
900
850
800
1000K
500K
0K
11 Oct
19
1 Nov
9
16
24
1 Dec
8
15
22
3 Jan
10
17
24
1 Feb
8
15
22
2 Mar
9
16
24
1 Apr

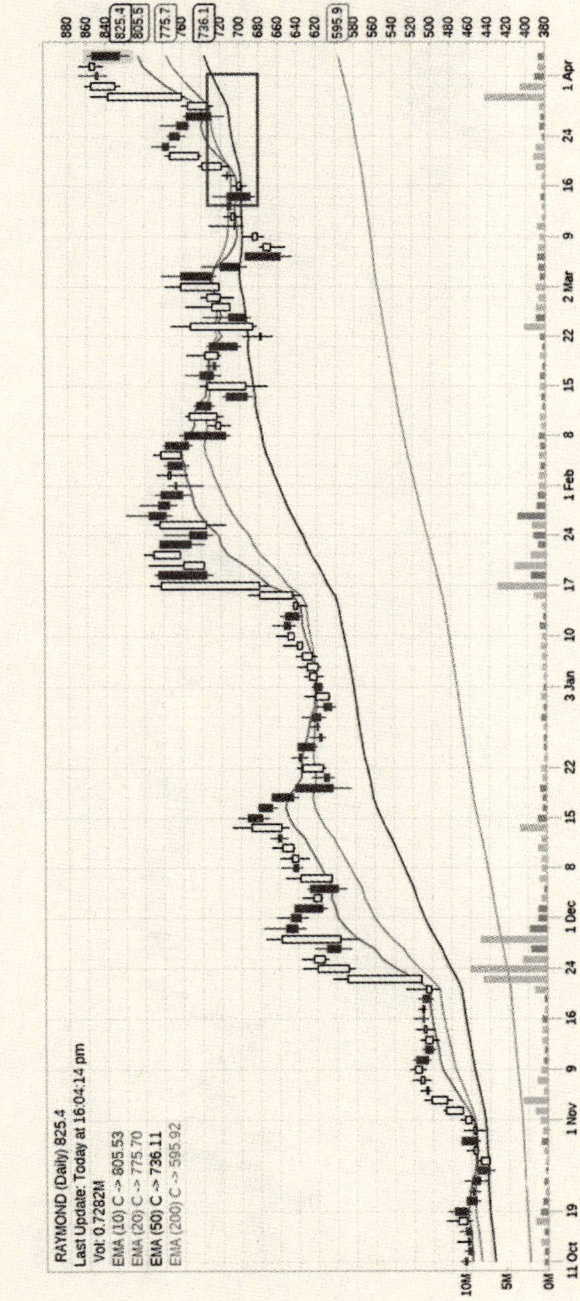
RAYMOND (Daily) 825.4
Last Update: Today at 16:04:14 pm
Vol: 0.7282M
EMA (10) C -> 805.53
EMA (20) C -> 775.70
EMA (50) C -> 736.11
EMA (200) C -> 595.92

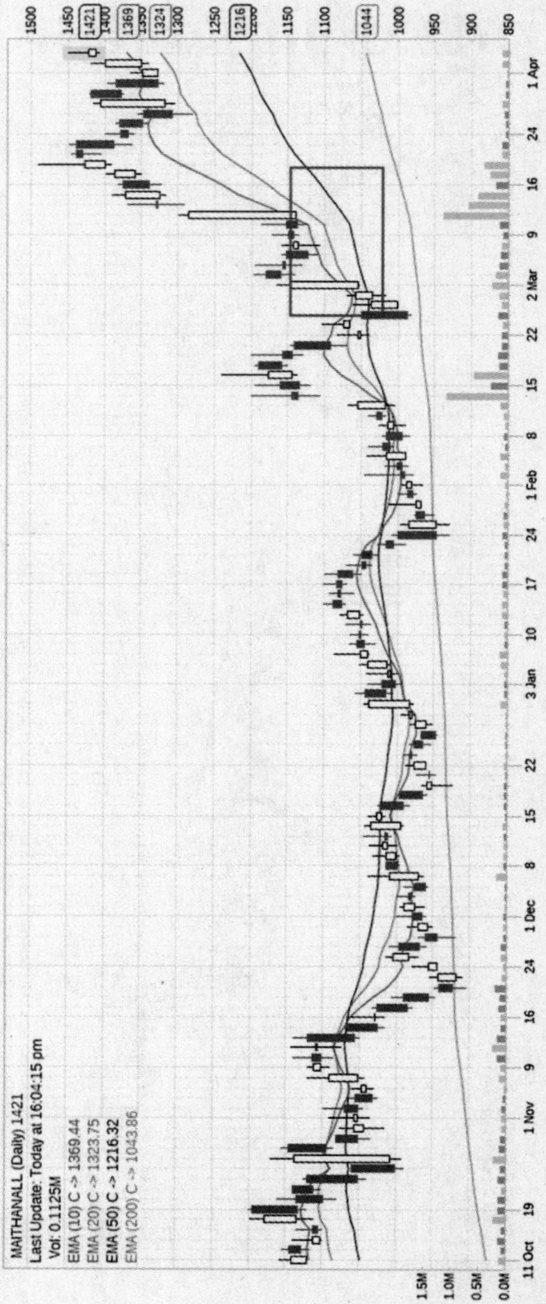
MAITHANALL (Daily) 1421
Last Update: Today at 16:04:15 pm
Vol: 0.1125M
EMA (10) C -> 1369.44
EMA (20) C -> 1323.75
EMA (50) C -> 1216.32
EMA (200) C -> 1043.86

STRATEGY 9

TRAP THE SHORT SELLERS

Shorting in a stock is exactly opposite of buying a stock, while shorting a stock we first sell it in anticipation of its price going down, As per the current market mechanism a trader can short sell a stock even without owning it. There can be various reasons behind short selling a particular share but the objective is very simple. The trader is expecting a downturn in stocks and wants to take advantage of that downturn by first selling it and then buying at a lesser price.

While discussing about shorts we must understand the concept of short squeeze also. It is a situation which goes against the expectation of the trader means that he has sold the stock anticipating that the prices will go down but the stock does opposite of it and there is a sharp increase in the price.

In February 2022, Indiamart shares were sold short heavily obvious reason was general market was down. On the date of expiry 24 February 2022 Nifty was down. In last 30 minutes of expiry cash market price of Indiamart rose Rs.400 from 4400 to 4800 while March 2022 future was still traded at Rs. 4300. India Mart is an extreme of Short seller's trap. Similar short squeezes happen at every month's expiry, but are smaller in magnitude. In this chapter, you will learn how to recognize and trade them. In this case a short seller need to cover his short of February at Rs.4800 and if he wanted to rollover it to next month he has to sell March future at Rs. 4300 which was more than 10% downside.

The ground level strategy

1. Market environment study is very important to work in this strategy, the kind of environment which we can find just after a correction or there may be any other reason that is why most trader in market expect stock to fall. A trader must search those stocks which are very less liquid in market trades and very highly active in terms of shorting, these kind of stock might have heavy active positions in terms of shorts by trader. These are ideal candidates for this strategy

2. Price of share must be at least Rs. 300/-

3. Average daily trading volume must be at least Rs. 1 Cr

4. Reason behind selecting a low float stock is that highly liquid stocks always allow a lot market participants to trade in it and big player or market maker can Influence the price in the opposite direction of what general trader think.

We can understand the concept of float and short float in following manner.

If we divide open interest with total free float we can get short quantity. In simple words total outstanding shares are those which can be traded daily without regulatory permission or restricted by time duration, restricted shares are generally promoters' shares, Pledged or any other category where regulatory permissions are required.

How it works:

People always short a stock because they have conviction that the stock is going to face a downtrend in upcoming days. They sell at current price and wait for the stock price to go down to cover it, covering simply means to buy the stock which the trader has sold earlier. But does it always go that easy? Is it that simple? Answer is of course a no, sometime the trader takes a call too early to short sell the stock before confirming the trend in which the stock is. Sometime there are other reasons by which the stock behaves in opposite manner and traces higher levels. Covering of a stock is triggered by two obvious reasons:

1. The stock is in position of short sell to trap and racing towards higher and higher levels.

2. The stock has reached the anticipated level and the trader looking for more to break or some smart trader start booking profits, which leads price to higher level.

The reverse event most of the time happens during quarterly earnings of companies where the trader tries to decode the results at the earliest in order to get first mover advantage and the price momentum backfires. Even whenever a market maker find that he has lot of long trade he can easily trap the short seller and force them to cover. You can find such stocks on the final settlement day of future and option every month. Some smart day trader can find it on daily basis on cash market when any stock goes up more than 12% and at the closing time after 3.15 pm you can find more fireworks in the stock.

Base mindset

The best time to adopt a short squeeze strategy where short sellers are trapped is when the market is in confirmed uptrend and there has been a recent correction. A confirmed market uptrend is when all major stocks trade above their 50 day moving averages and their 10/20 day exponential moving averages. The major stock indexes are- large caps (NIFTY), mid-caps (Midcap Index) and small caps (Small cap Index). In such situation many traders find stocks in overbought level which attract them to short the stock which seems quite extended.

On the other hand, a major correction is when the major indices or broader markets have faced more than 10% corrections. Once the market has reached to the level of 10% correction the trader must stop himself and look for certain signs of stocks bottoming.

In recent market uptrends you will find a lot of traders who are happily sitting on heavy short positions because they are sitting on profitable positions which were created earlier when the market was in a downtrend. To use this strategy, we need to take advantage of this comfort situation of short trader as the stocks are about to go higher and the new entrant might make money due to short squeeze positions.

To get the best out of this strategy we need to be perfect in terms of timing of entering into stocks, it's on the extreme side of top and bottom of the market for a suggested short squeeze strategy:

1. When the market is on its new multiyear high and most of the short traders are tired of holding the short and losing whole lot of money.

2. When the market is around its low where short traders are making a lot of money and market trend is about to see a reversal.

Look for the place to enter

In general, there are two strategic point to enter in the stock, First is when it is a confirmed uptrend or second when it is oversold. A short selling trader has done this because he wants to sell higher and buy lower and make money from this, but when the stocks are at new multi-year and there seems to be no stopping, the short seller are forced to cover the positions which further pushes the stock prices even higher. A stock when in confirmed uptrend will in general repeat the near historical performance, the one which has gone up around 50 to 75% will not hesitate in going upwards another 50 to 75% in coming days or weeks, and it's a fantastic play to be in the strategy we are discussing here.

On the other hand, there are stocks which would take a breather after falling a lot, say 50 to 75%, the stock would take a correction in their bearish trend and would give bounce to implement short squeeze strategy to trap the short seller because of being in an oversold category. A recent example of this is newly Listed Zomato which after touching an all-time high of Rs. 169 corrected up to the level of Rs. 76 in 2022 and after that trend reversed and stock went up to Rs. 87 again.

The stoploss- yes it's the most important part!

The initial stop must be around 0.5% below the lows of the entry day or right below the stock's 10-day EMA or 20-day EMA.

Look at the quantity and risk capital

The volume depends on the amount of money you are ready to take to markets. In general, a trader must not take position of more than 1% of risk to your total capital. Also if you are a new investor, for this strategy specifically risk not more than 0.50% of your capital.

Exit at the right point

A swing trade taken under this strategy can be squared off in two tranches, the first half of the position can be liquidated in next 2.5 to 8 days and the second half can be done when the stock on its upward path closes below its 10/20 days EMA.

Another exiting strategy can be to follow the stock for next 2.5 weeks when the stock keep rising. Here, you must look at the range of the third week which essentially must be larger than earlier two weeks.

What is it all about!

We must know and understand that a short seller is equally important part of the system, he cannot do this activity without any base, and somewhere the short seller has find out or perceived that there is a gap between the company's current market value and actual value embedded in the business. In its analysis the trade is right but what he is evaluating is a long term perspective and here, we are not looking for any very long term trade. In short term the short seller is wrong more time than he is right.

Another scenario is about the future growth of the stock, where a growth stock is always market favourite and very soon it is going to find a buyer for itself. The current shorts in the market paves the way for future buying and that may prove the talked about as a great strategy.

One most important aspect to remember is that short squeeze is not a very long term strategy and the trader trading with this must not try to prove himself right in a long term, it's a swing trade and profits must be taken off table with a disciplined timeline.

STRATEGY 10

MEAN MEANS A LOT- WORKING ON MEAN REVERSAL STRATEGY

Most of the time while travelling, catching a highway or a straight road to the destination is the most rewarding thing, you will reach to the destination for sure but searching for a short cut is not a bad things You don't know if you can save a lot of fuel as well reach to the destination faster than anticipation.

While driving in stock markets also going with the wind always rewards the trader provided that the trader judges the direction well, but sometime taking contra call are too good to avoid. It may make faster money than routine trading.

The ground level strategy

A trader can be rewarded with bottom fishing provided the following strategy is taken care of:

1. Search for the beaten down stocks which are at multi month low but in a day's trade closing on greener part as well as at the day's high.
2. When you buy these stock at around day end your stop loss to be at the low for the day and target can be declining 50 day simple moving average.

3. Once the market correction is done and it starts recovering, these kinds of stock can deliver somewhere around 25 to 75% gains. Which is far better than any going with the wind strategy.

RS (Relative Strength) can be used for measuring momentum divergences. An RS measures the speed and change of price movement in a stock or index. It indicates momentum of a stock or index. These kind of indicators can be seen on various charting platforms. A trader must remember that the pricing follows the momentum in terms of topping and bottoming.

Let us understand something on Positive and negative divergence of a stock. Suppose a stock is making a multi month high but the bullish momentum is not yet confirmed, it's a state of negative divergence. This divergence can lead to a sudden change in trend and can lead to the stock from being an uptrend to shifting towards a downtrend.

On the other hand without getting confirmation by momentum indicator if the stocks hits a multi month low it's a state of positive momentum divergence. This divergence can take the stock from a downtrend to an uptrend which is kind of trend reversal pattern.

How it works

Mean reversion is based on a theory that the most trodden down stock will be the best performer in the coming days. Keep checking for stocks which denies to go down further even when there is a solid reason to go down or bad news, it is sign that stock is very near to its bottom. For example, if the crude oil shots up from 90 to 130 dollars and Asian Paints does not go down even in that news, there is something to note down.

When the short sellers start working on a recovery it can trigger a real larger rally. Which will be even faster and bigger than a bull phase.

Base mindset

If the broader market and all the major indices are above 50 day moving averages then the trend is greatly bullish and the market has a clear cut trend. In this kind of market if you try to go against the trend and try to take a contrarian call it might cost you a lot of money. Contrarian mean reversal strategy do not work in trending market. Never fight the market. Market is far bigger than you or me or any trader in the market.

Look for range bound markets which will give you lot of contrarian opportunities, in this kind of market the major once are like Sensex and NIFTY trades above 50 DMA and the other indices like small cap and mid caps trades below 50 DMA. Look for high momentum stocks which have surged more than 75 to 100 percent in last one year. These stocks are easy breakdown candidates when the market is range bound as described above.

If we talk about bottoming out of the market, we must understand the concept of forced liquidation first. Forced liquidation is state when the traders are forced to sell as they are left with no other options either due to emotional reason or margin pressure from broker. At this stage some of the good short sellers enter in the market in expectation of continuation of trend, this is the stage of bottoming out for the market and leads towards a major reversal stage. This reversal sometime can be carried over for so many days.

After a major market correction there are two category of future winners first is those which had a free fall and everyone wanted to get rid of those, and the other ones which performed the best. The first category is the best to work on the mean reversal strategy. The second we discussed in relative strength strategy.

Checking some of the recent examples about these stocks is Lemon Tree Hotels, during the crash of 2020 when COVID struck the market and there was a complete ban on travel and tourism the stock crashed from Rs. 62 to Rs.17 and barely survived. Just within May 2020 to Dec 2020 the stock zoomed to more than 100 percent as the government started lifting COVID restriction and stocks like Lemon Tree and Indian Hotels started performing. PVR, Inox and Indigo started performing as soon as there was a feeling in the market about opening of economy. When Complete opening theme started playing out and stocks which performed in lock down like Pharma started weakening.

The stoploss- yes it's the most important part!

Look for the price targets near 50 or 200 DMA of the stock and the stoploss to be kept at the day's low when you bought the stock.

Look at the quantity and risk capital

This strategy can give you big returns but it's a bit risky also, so always bet not more than that .5% to 1% of your risk capital. Remember, we are about to trade a highly volatile stock which can turn either ways so cautious trades are advised.

Exit at the right point

Look for mean reversing strategy to buy and the same strategy to exit also. Targets for exiting can be around 10 to 20% of buying price.

What is it all about!

Mean reversal happens in the market but these may not always lead towards a clear cut trend. Sometime, mean reversal stands for a consolidation phase which remain for days. There are a lot of traders waiting on the side-lines which want to bottom fish.

There are a lot of traders who buy the stock near top to play momentum. So always looking for a clear cut trend is only rewarding.

Identifying a stock for mean reversing is not an easy task, we must always remember that while going up the stocks are so individual but while going down there are a lot of friends. Never try to buy dips in any stock if the stock is making multi month low in general bull market. So try to be safe while doing bottom fishing.

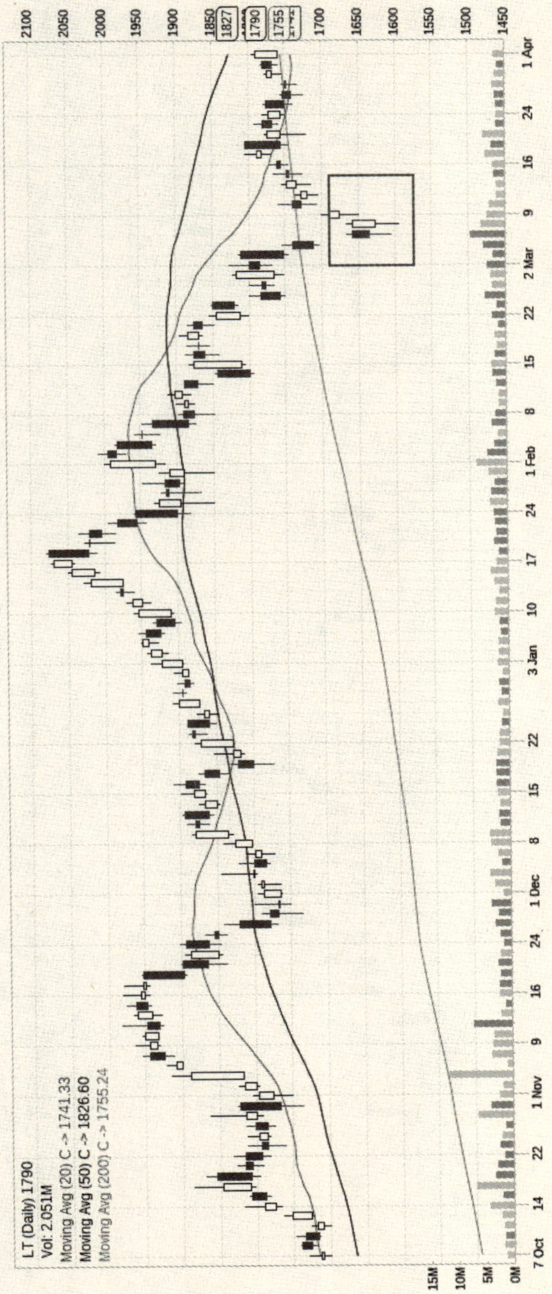
LT (Daily) 1790
Vol: 2.051M
Moving Avg (20) C -> 1741.33
Moving Avg (50) C -> 1826.60
Moving Avg (200) C -> 1755.24

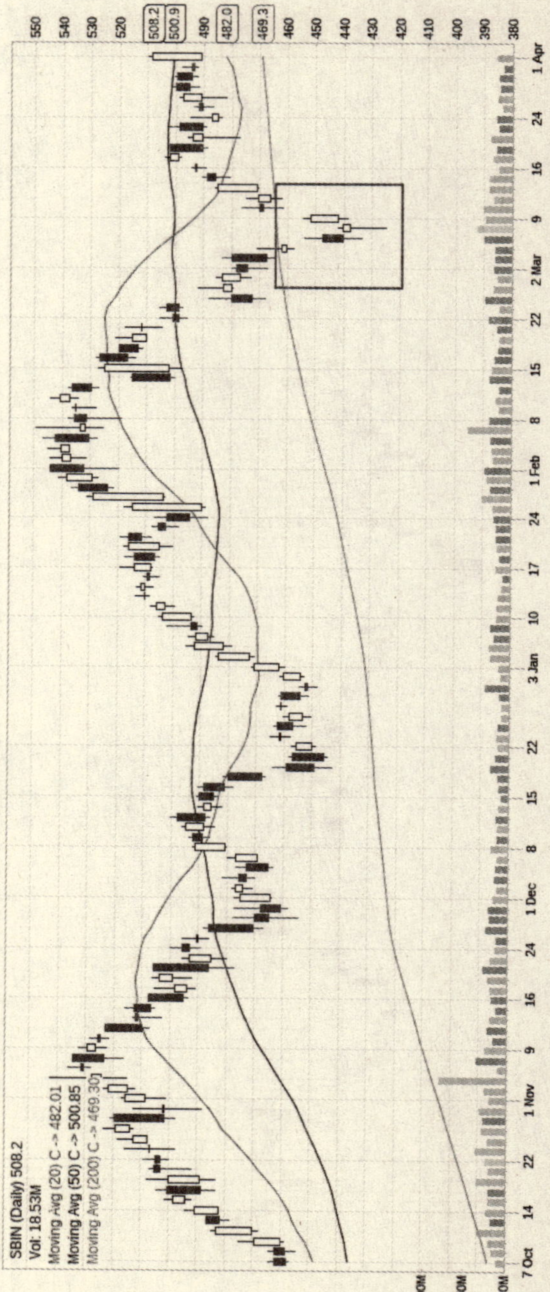
SBIN (Daily) 508.2
Vol: 18.53M
Moving Avg (20) C -> 482.01
Moving Avg (50) C -> 500.85
Moving Avg (200) C -> 469.30

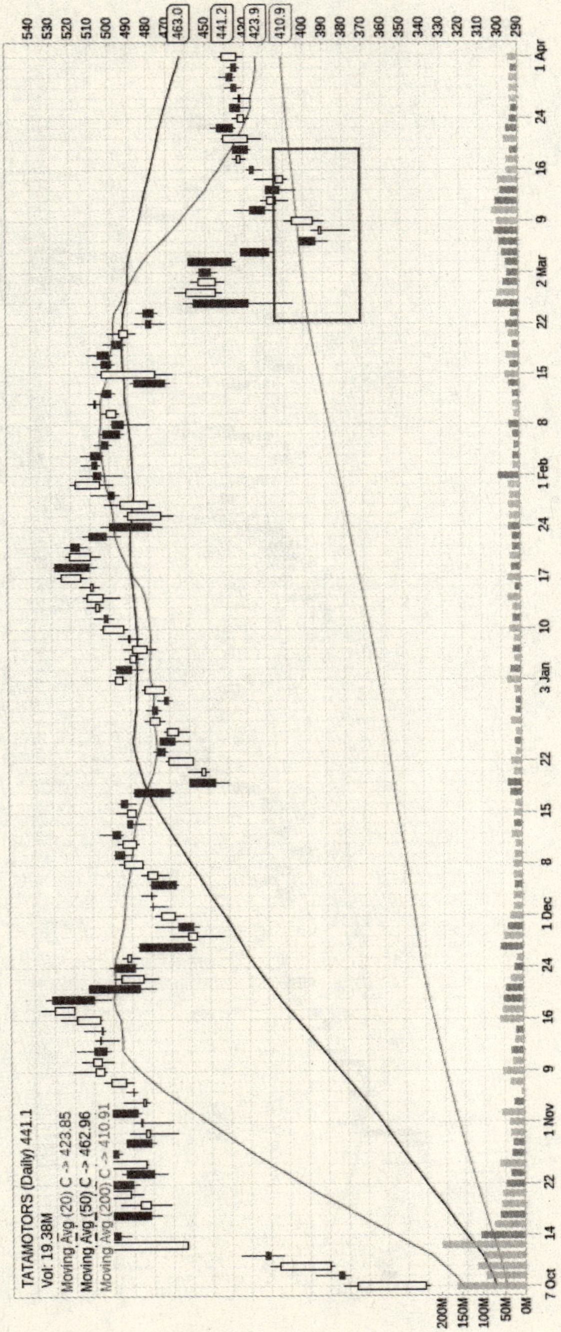
TATAMOTORS (Daily) 441.1
Vol: 19.38M
Moving Avg (20) C -> 423.85
Moving Avg (50) C -> 462.96
Moving Avg (200) C -> 410.91

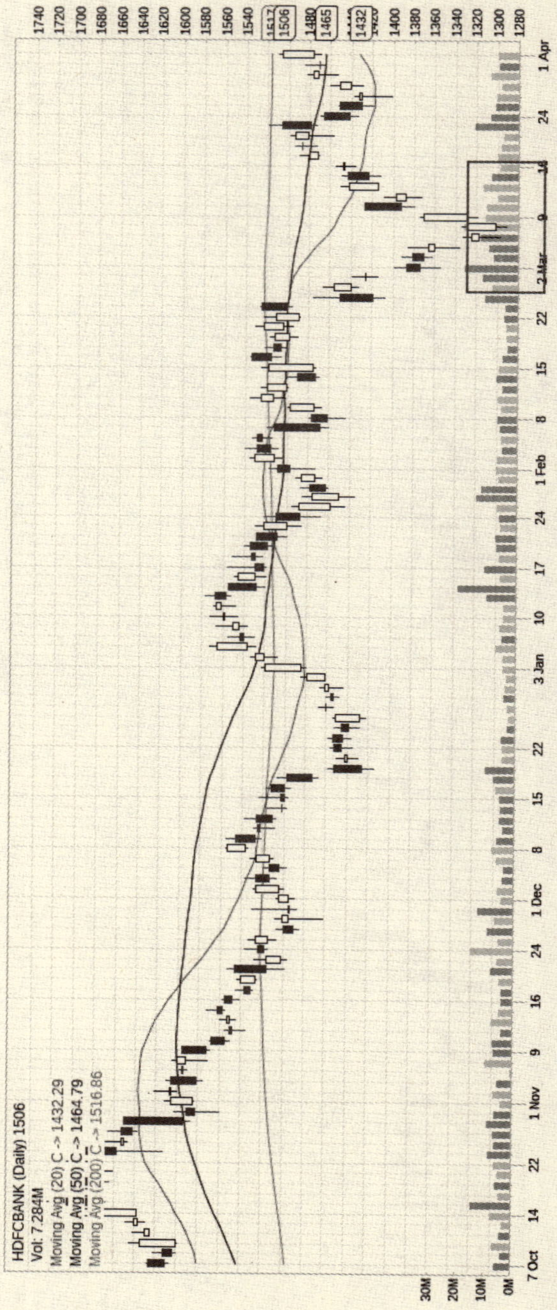
HDFCBANK (Daily) 1506
Vol: 7.284M
Moving Avg (20) C -> 1432.29
Moving Avg (50) C -> 1464.79
Moving Avg (200) C -> 1516.86

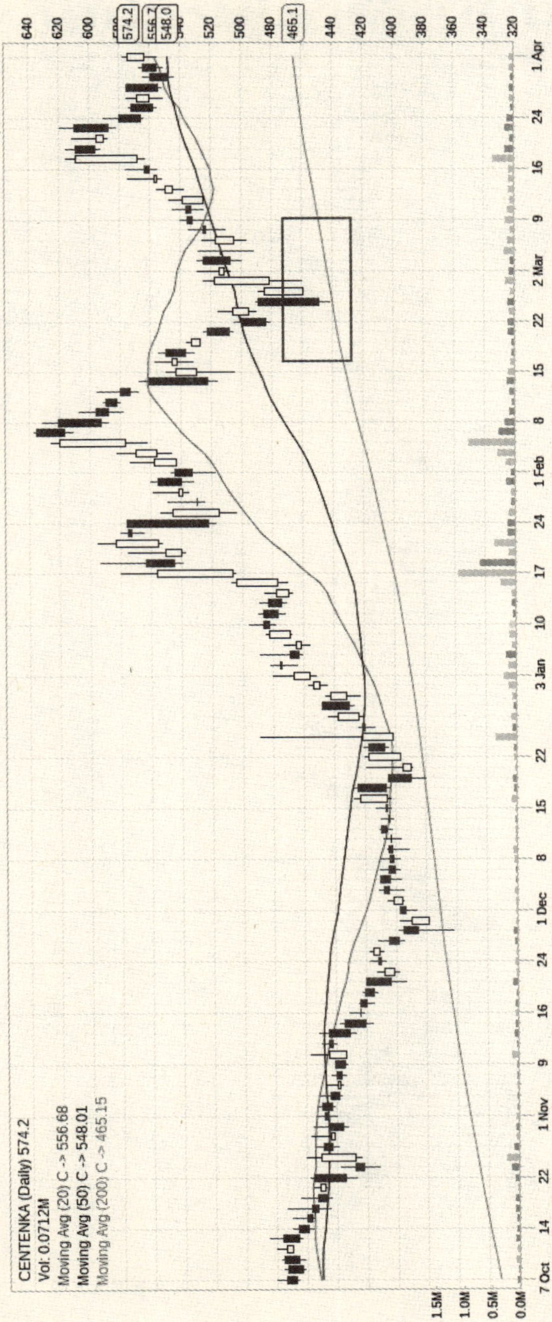
CENTENKA (Daily) 574.2
Vol: 0.0712M
Moving Avg (20) C -> 556.68
Moving Avg (50) C -> 548.01
Moving Avg (200) C -> 465.15
574.2
556.7
548.0
465.1
640
620
600
520
500
480
440
420
400
380
360
340
320
1.5M
1.0M
0.5M
0.0M
7 Oct
14
22
1 Nov
9
16
24
1 Dec
8
15
22
3 Jan
10
17
24
1 Feb
8
15
22
2 Mar
9
16
24
1 Apr

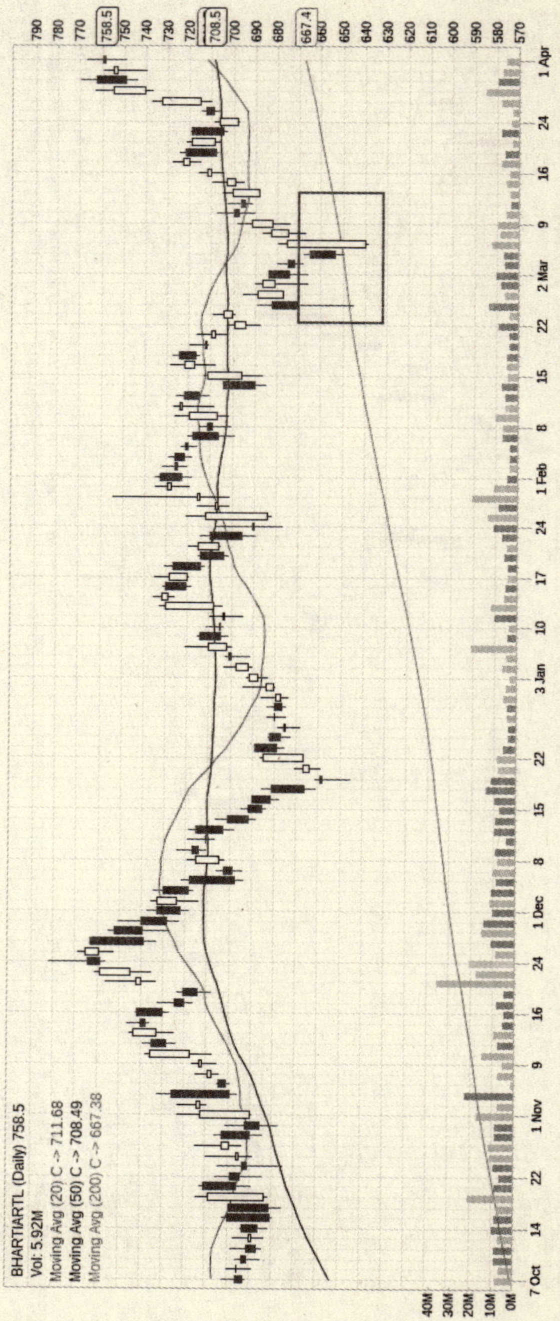
BHARTIARTL (Daily) 758.5
Vol: 5.92M
Moving Avg (20) C -> 711.68
Moving Avg (50) C -> 708.49
Moving Avg (200) C -> 667.38

STRATEGY 11

SUPPORT AND RESISTANCE-THE PLACE WHERE STOCKS TAKE A HALT

Support and resistance level's understanding is a real great tool for all type of traders, we all know that a lot of time in a year the stock goes range bound and this range is in between support and resistance. When the range bound trade is at its resistance level then the trend tends to be Bearish on the other side if the prices are at support level then the trend is towards Bull zone. The logic is very simple, the support level prices gives buyer support or short covering which gives a boost to price & volume and vice-versa.

A widespread knowledge of support and resistance level keeps the traders busy to be ready to sell when the stock is at its resistance because the market knows that the stock has very less probability of going up further up on the other hand if Bulls keep waiting to buy the stock when it's at its support level because going down is not a probable scenario.

The ground level strategy

The trader must learn that support and resistance level never work on even numbers, most of the traders in market seems to be obsessed with even number nearing to zeroes. For instance, while discussing the Sensex level we always discuss like 50,000 or 60,000, but the charts don't go like this, it might work on 51285 or 59395. It is so good for individual stocks also, the resistance for reliance will never be 3200 exact or support will never be at exact 3000. This is very unlikely scenario. The chartist must learn to find exact resistance and support level. This will give better understanding to find out swing trade opportunities.

How it works

First of all, the trader must identify the support and resistance level, once this exercise is done swing trades must be taken if not exactly on these level then closest to those. Chances of making more money is there if you close the trade nearest to the levels. One more mistake which some of the traders are trapped into is that while buying or selling a particular stock they work on limit orders which is not a good strategy to be in. there is always ample margin for a swing trader where he can afford to execute trades on market orders. Remember the swing trade is to make fine amount of money and not to work on some basis points. But yes if your quantity is huge then obviously putting multiple limit orders is a better strategy.

The stop loss is another important part of this strategy, once triggered it must not be missed. A swing trader's strategy here must be to make more of good trades which makes money and less of bad trades which is a loss making scenario. Don't expect to make money on every trade. It will not be possible. The greed of making money all the time is the worst enemy of a trader. Set a boundary of support and resistance and be strict about those, don't try your luck too much and let the numbers do their job.

Base mindset

Best time to use it is in the range bound market. In such a market a lot of stocks goes into consolidation or flat base pattern and it is the best time to use this strategy. So here basically we are playing the consolidation period or trading between the flat base pattern formations. Base or resistance can be easily used for first 2-3 times but always remember as a particular base or resistance becomes weak on 4th time onwards.

Look for the place to enter

Support and resistance levels are never constant, with the change in pricing of the stock the support and resistance level will keep changing. If we analyse these levels well then we will be able to identify the range in which we have to work, this trading range is the commandment for a trader. One important part of the story is that sometime the stock will cross the resistance level and sometime it will break down below the support level. In both the scenarios we will have to change the trading range and if already entered a trade then have to follow strict stop loss.

If the stock breaks the resistance level with higher highs and higher lows than the trend is shifted to upward and the old trading range must be re-adjusted. On the other side if the stock breaks below the support level with lower highs and lower lows then the trend is shifted to bearish zone and the trading range must be adjusted accordingly. When as a trader if you observe a horizontal trend line begin to break again and again on one side, it can be an early sign of the side of the stock's range where there can be next breakout and you might have to follow for a new support and resistance levels.

The stoploss- yes it's the most important part!

The stoploss must be kept at a close below the lowest price in that support zone.

Price support signal parameters

1. A price support is tested again and again.
2. Price of a stock hitting previous support zone and holding it out is always a buy zone.
3. Stocks pricing breaks the support level but it enters again to the range of support and resistance, it's also a place to buy.

Look at the quantity and risk capital

At this strategy we will keep the risk at 1% of the total capital for every trade.

Exit at the right point

1. Book your profits when the ratio of price to the stoploss is 2 to 3 times.
2. Maximum profit target is set at returning to the upper resistance zone.

What is it all about!

In routine trade you will always find a lot of charts which will be range bound and trading sideways. These are perfect candidate to take a swing trade. These kind of stocks will always give you perfect levels of support and resistance levels. If the stock crosses the trading range and does it for two consecutive days than we will look for another range bound opportunity. Here a trader must always take care that he knows the clear cut difference between the stock's trend and its trading range as it is very crucial for buying support and selling resistance.

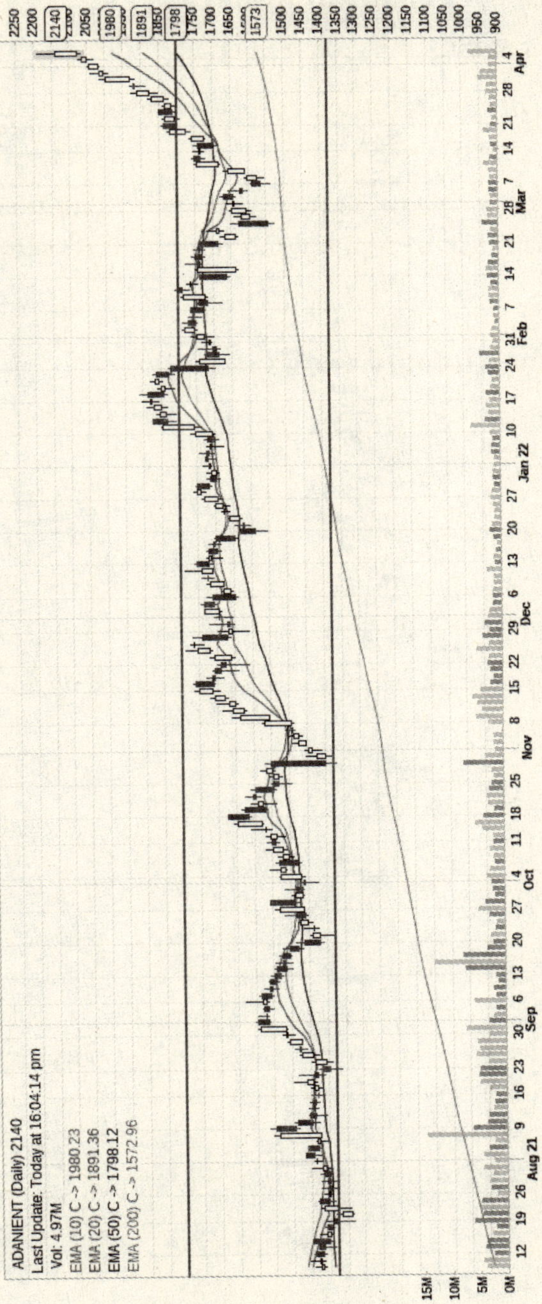
ADANIENT (Daily) 2140
Last Update: Today at 16:04:14 pm
Vol: 4.97M
EMA (10) C -> 1980.23
EMA (20) C -> 1891.36
EMA (50) C -> 1798.12
EMA (200) C -> 1572.96

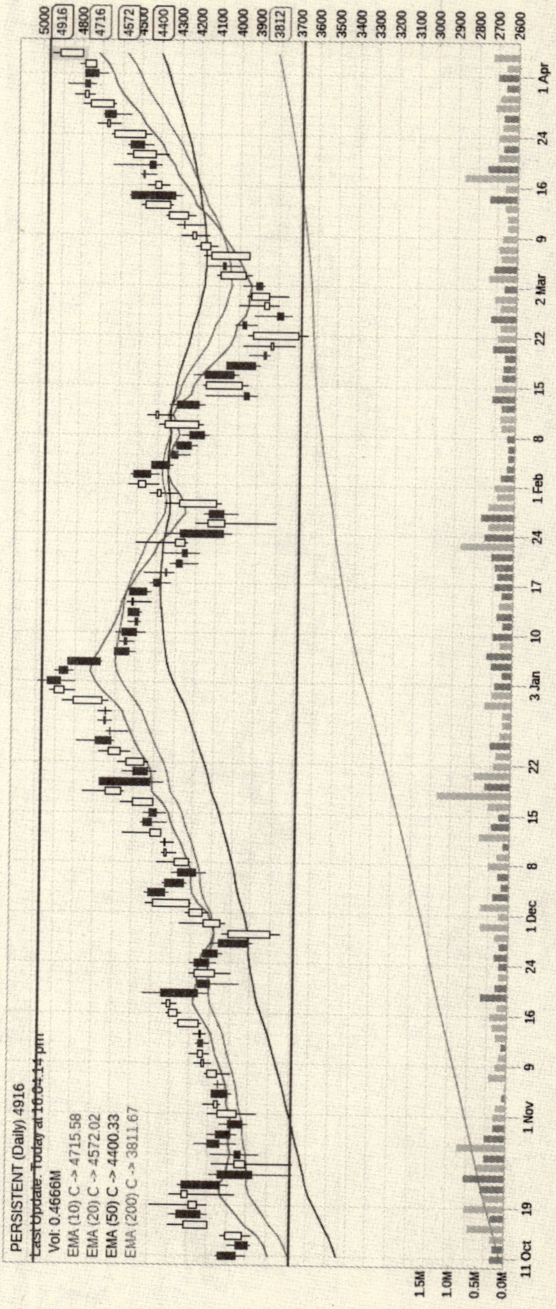
PERSISTENT (Daily) 4916
Last Update: Today at 16:04:14 pm
Vol: 0.4666M
EMA (10) C -> 4715.58
EMA (20) C -> 4572.02
EMA (50) C -> 4400.33
EMA (200) C -> 3811.67

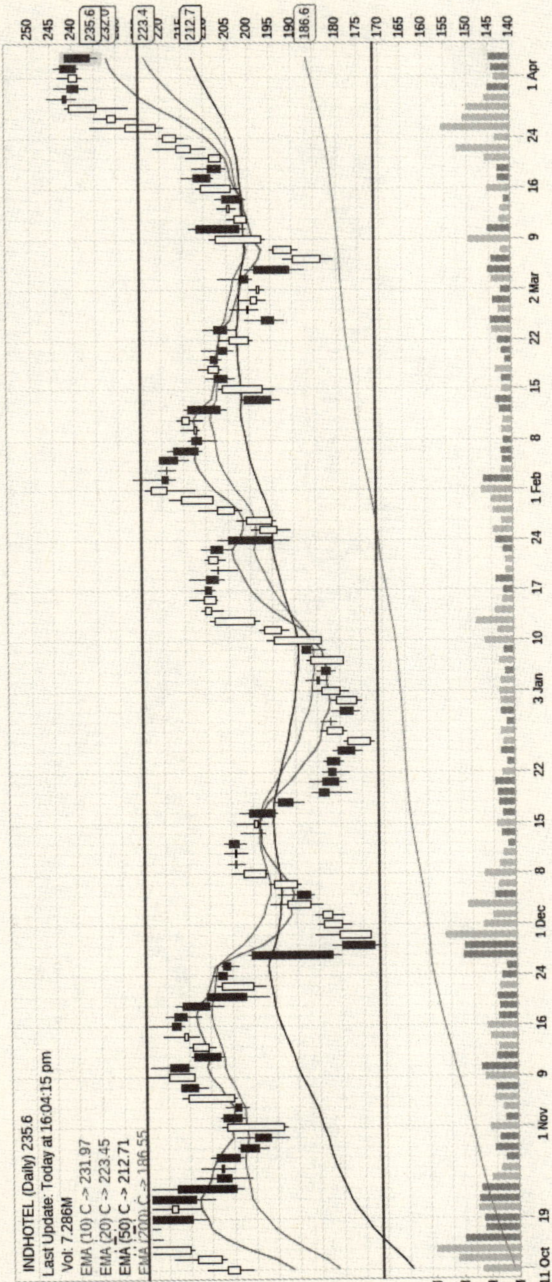
INDHOTEL (Daily) 235.6
Last Update: Today at 16:04:15 pm
Vol: 7.286M
EMA (10) C -> 231.97
EMA (20) C -> 223.45
EMA (50) C -> 212.71
EMA (200) C -> 186.55

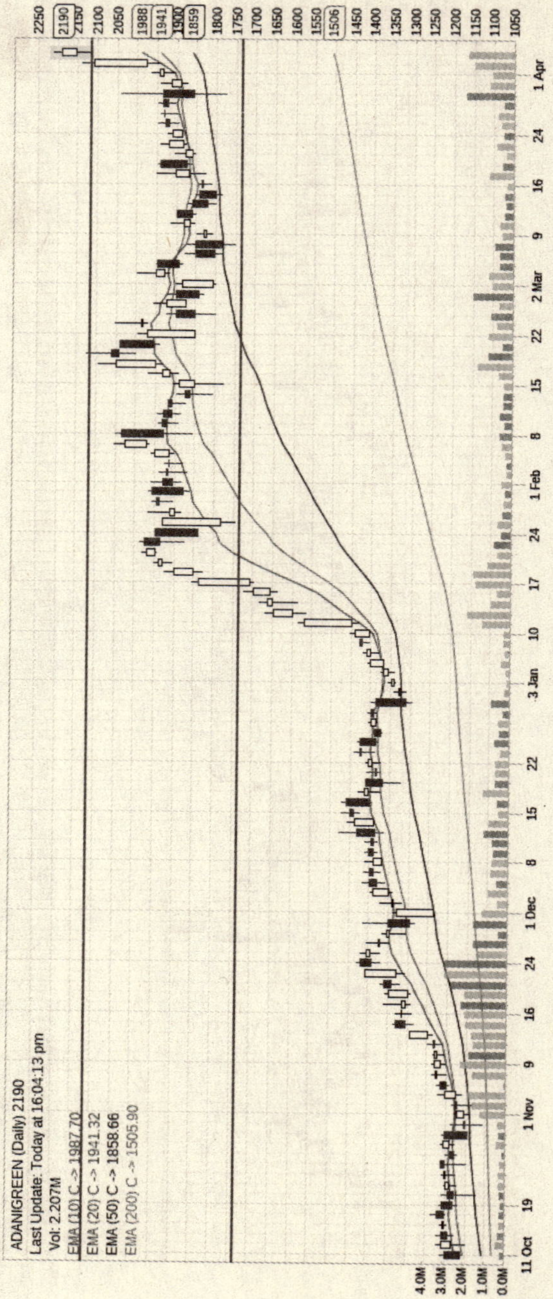
ADANIGREEN (Daily) 2190
Last Update: Today at 16:04:13 pm
Vol: 2.207M
EMA (10) C -> 1987.70
EMA (20) C -> 1941.32
EMA (50) C -> 1858.66
EMA (200) C -> 1505.90

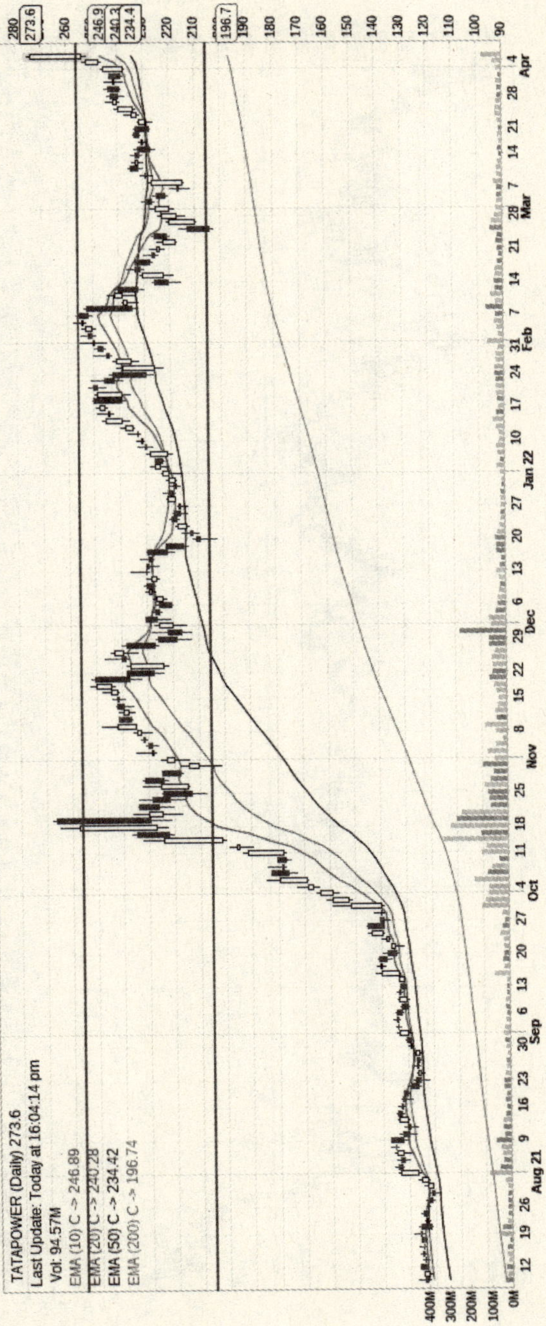
TATAPOWER (Daily) 273.6
Last Update: Today at 16:04:14 pm
Vol: 94.57M
EMA (10) C -> 246.89
EMA (20) C -> 240.28
EMA (50) C -> 234.42
EMA (200) C -> 196.74

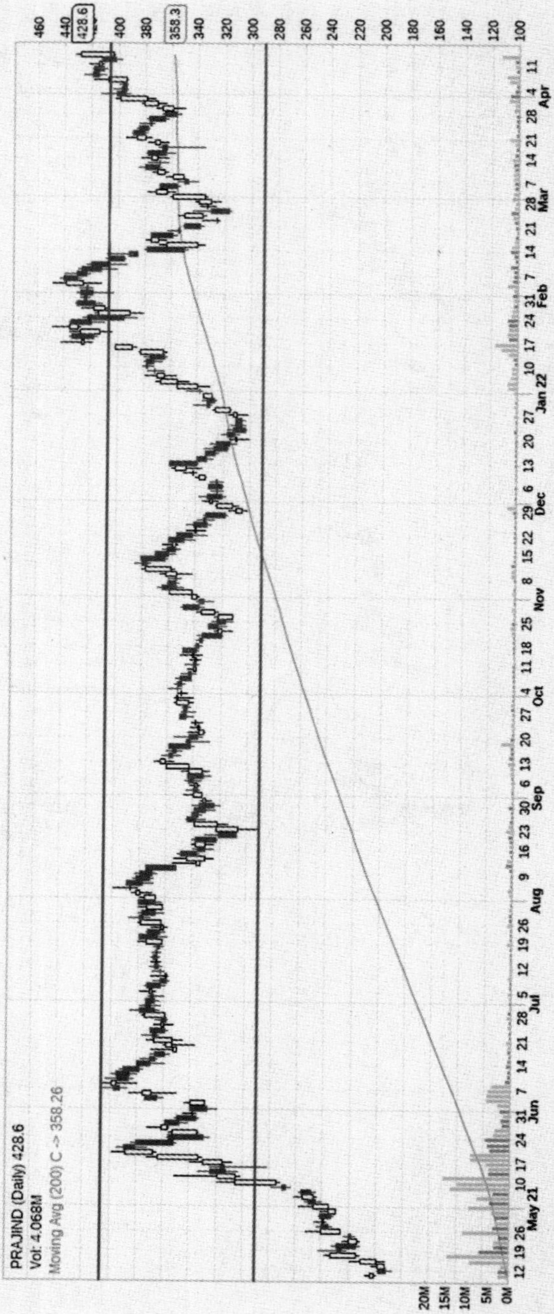
PRAJIND (Daily) 428.6
Vol: 4.068M
Moving Avg (200) C -> 358.26

STRATEGY 12

OFS & BULK DEALS

OFS and bulk deals are very regular as well as very important part of the stock market trading mechanism. It is very important because large investors or promoters are involved in it. Through these kinds of deals the investors or promoters sell from a range of .5 to 5% stake in the companies. In recent times in 2022 there have been a lot of bulk deals in some of the biggest names. Carlyl sold 2.78% in SBI cards for around 2229 crore, Invesco sold 7.74% in Zee entertainment for 2092 crore and Canada Pension funds sold 2.02% in Kotak bank for 7079 crore. On the other hand Govt. is also a very regular participants in OFS (Offer for Sale) where it offers its stake in PSUs, generally at a discount to the current market price. Recently Govt. raised 3000 crore while selling 1.5% stake in ONGC.

One of the most important part of these kinds of deals is that these deals are to be announced in advance and to be notified to the exchanges earlier than the day of trade. This at large decides the day's trading mood. In general the stocks trades lower on the trading day as the market is in selling mode rather than buying.

The News

Largely it is about buying the rumour and selling on the news. Another recent example of this which is not essentially a bulk deal but a large trade of share in HDFC and HDFC bank which will be one of the largest merger in the history of Indian corporate world. The duo will create an entity worth 14 lac crore after the merge and is going to be a financial and corporate powerhouse. No doubt both of the stock hit the roof on the day merge was announced.

Another story of buying in rumour and selling on news is of Zee entertainment, where the stock crashed due to Invesco's intervention and within very few day the stock skyrocketed with huge price and volume action and when the merger was announced with Sony.

The ground level strategy

Under the strategy of trading bulk deals we are in generally looking for an induced swing trade opportunity where there is an opportunity due to the news created by the bulk deal activity. Keep looking for these kind of news floating in the markets. In general local market intelligence will have this information quite before the news is announced and that starts reflecting in the stock price few days before the actual deal day.

Another important part of the strategy is that here we are looking for those companies which are fundamentally sound and the activity of bulk deal is not only about someone exiting and its pessimism but also about some strong hands buying and being optimistic about the share.

Base mindset

The basic theory behind any bulk deal is an institutional activity where a particular large investor holding the share for long wants to exit because of following reasons:

1. Stock target is achieved and the investors under its strategy does not want to hold the stock anymore.
2. Feud with the management are not very common issues but we witnessed it in the Zee-Invesco deal.

3. For government, the OFS are a tool to raise instant money where it saves itself from coming up with an FPO.

Look for the place to enter

In general the block deals are done below 4 to 6% discount to the current market price of the stock. In layman terms you may call it large buyer's discount. We must look for an entry in the stock the lower part of the range. For instance the bulk deal in Kotak was done with a price range of 1681.26 to 1769.75. Which was at a 0 to 5% discount to the earlier day's closing price of 1769.75. Investors must have tried to enter the stock at around 1681 in best case if not then even 1700 would be a great bargain.

Another alternative strategy that can be adopted when the stock starts grinding lower few days before the bulk deal day. It happens because there is always an insider news about the event to happen. If you enter at that time also it can be a good value buy.

On 13th April 2022 SBI Mutual Fund bought 33 lakh shares of Mrs Bectors Food at Rs 303 per share. Shares were sold by GW Crown Pte among others. Stock was trading 372 on 7th April just four days earlier to bulk deal. Even it was closed 337 just one day before the bulk deal on 12th April. Average trade price was 307 just after bulk deal. You as a swing trader should be buying stock around 307 with intraday target of 3%. Happy to share stock traded 325 by after noon given swing trader a chance to earn easy 3% intraday. You can check it on hourly chart and understand the complete process.

The Stoploss- yes it's the most important part!

It is usually seen that under the strategy when we are trading bulk deals and OFS the stoploss is not triggered as once the pressure of bulk deal is lifted the stock starts showing in an upward move but keeping stoploss is always necessary. Under this strategy stop loss will be at 2% below the price of bulk deal, for those who are trading intraday this can be 1% below the bulk deal.

Look at the quantity and risk capital

A trader must bet not more than that .5% to 1% of your risk capital on trades based on bulk deal.

Exit at the right point

If the stock maintains its WATP (Weighted Average Trading Price) then holding it for longer is not a bad choice. In this strategy in general we are looking for around 6% gains in 2. 5 to 5 days and for intraday trader the gains are targeted at around 3%. Most of the time it is seen that the stock will generate targeted returns in the day of bulk deal itself. This happens because bulk deal is traded in fundamentally sound stock only and once the pressure of selling is done a fresh round of buying emerges which take the stock higher and makes swing trade very successful.

What is it all about!

Among all of the type of swing trading strategies, this particular is one of the easiest as the price range is not to be discovered by the trader, the price band is already known and the trader has to be disciplined and take care of stoplosses. Bulk deals are very regular in stock market and if you look at the exchanges websites, you will find data and details of all of the bulk deals done in the past. All the times the traders are well informed about the bulk deal in advance which means that it doesn't take the trader by surprise. It is a good money making exercise if we track it well and execute the buy order on time.

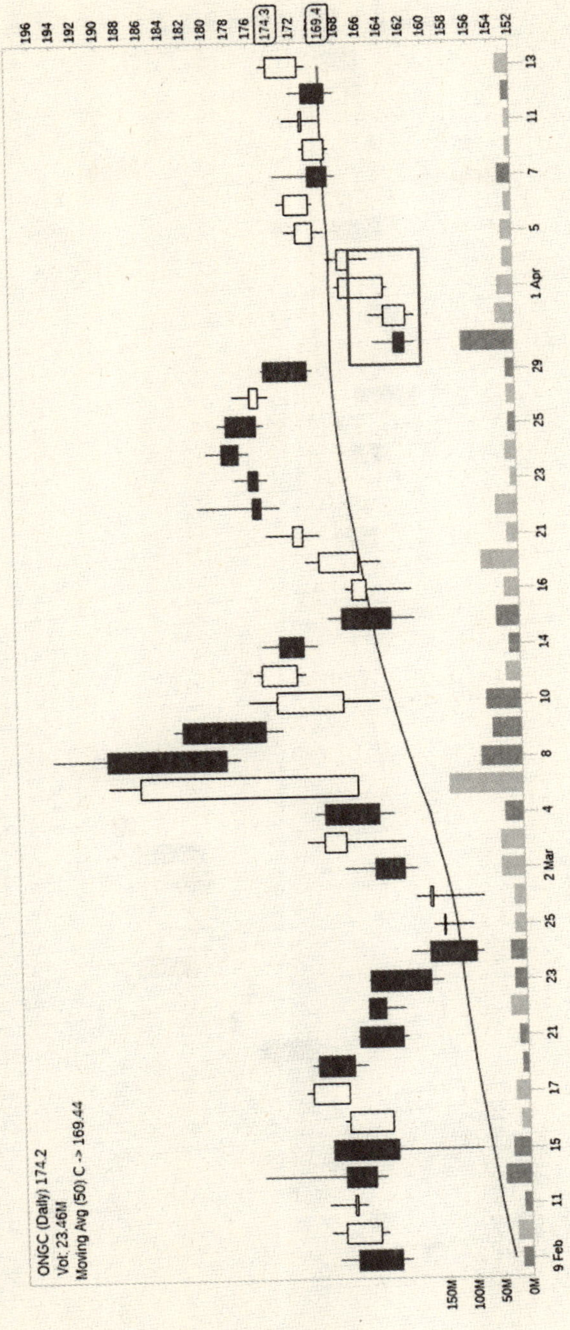
ONGC (Daily) 174.2
Vol: 23.46M
Moving Avg (50) C -> 169.44

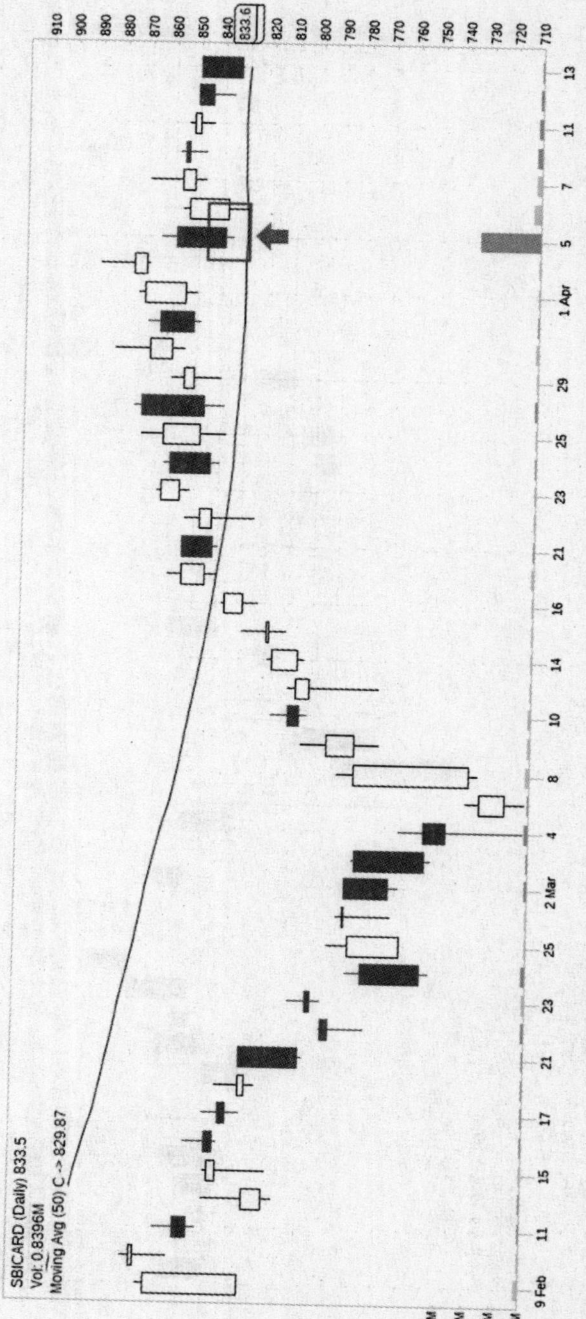
SBICARD (Daily) 833.5
Vol: 0.8396M
Moving Avg (50) C -> 829.87

STRATEGY 13

THE INDUSTRY- ONE PLUS ONE IS ELEVEN

As we know that money is always on the move, it cannot stay in a single house for very long time period. But, what's the type of house in which money find solace and comfort of stay? For sure the house is not named after few industry stocks. Money always finds its place in various industries, an industry essentially is a group of companies having similar line of business, like Telecom, Steel, Bank, Pharma and many more.

For so many years stock market around the globe has shown one clear cut trend that one single industry is not all time favourite, it's all cyclical. For few years metal will be favourite and for other year banks might be a peaceful destination. It's not very easy to catch the trend about an industry but it's less tough than finding momentum of a single stock.

Since COVID struck the world and after second wave of 2021 when economic recovery got into trend metal became everyone's favourite, especially in India we could see metal stocks tripling within a year. Same way at the early trend after COVID first wave Pharma became a sweet spot. Before the global meltdown of 2008 BFSI was the hot commodity and everyone's favourite around the globe.

In terms of industry trends defence is also dancing to the tune of growth, government's make in India vision and thrust on defence sector is giving huge fillip to stocks like BEML, Astra Micro and so many others. Another hot area is India's PLI scheme where Pharma and white goods manufacturer are tend to benefit also. Beneficiary will be companies like Dixon and Amber enterprises.

The ground level strategy

1. Keep looking for the best performing industry
2. See which stocks are industry leaders with earnings and price volume actions. A trader can buy pullbacks towards rising 10, 20 or 50 day EMAs.
3. Chose those stocks which are from the hot industry as well nearing around a breakout. This will give you double advantage.

Ways to identify the leading industries:

1. Keep looking for the economic scenarios and those industries which worked well in past few months, it will allow for an easy analysis.
2. Check the list of that group which is around a breakout as an industry, if you find any industry at that level it is time to choose individual stocks out of that group.
3. Past week's performance is important, look for those which are up more than 3 to 5 % in last week.
4. On a reverse approach look for those stocks which are breaking out and check the industry status.

Risk management is another advantage of trading an industry trend as trading in industry leaders is always less risky, in this strategy you are trading a broader trend which has less probability of going wrong.

If we see the recent market scenarios of 2022, since the beginning of year, the Oil companies are buzzing a lot, ONGC is ruling the market on higher oil prices and seems like it will continue the run, even the steel sector is having a dream run due to continuous rise in metal price. Tata Steel or JSW steel has doubled since April 2021. Power sector too is not standing still and stocks like Tata Power and JSW Energy have gained 50% from September 2021

How it works

So, when we are working on an industry strategy we need to understand a lot of data and activity behind it, Industry trends sometime may be very deceiving also, at times tech industry does it to investors. Always look for data about who is buying these stocks. Look for HNI and FII activities. As these trends are bought by those investors who wants to buy them for at least few months or years. This creates a ripple effect that skillful swing traders know how to use.

Every now and then there have been different theme working for market. A lot of internal and external factors do affect. Let's have a small journey to understand these kind of trends with respect to Indian stock markets. During the extreme Bull Run of 2003 to 2007 we saw a lot of government reforms in India and that gave a fillip to stocks like ONGC, Sesa Goa, SAIL etc, In short we saw a great momentum in government owned companies. Few years earlier than this during 1996 to 1999

Internet stocks went to the roof. The theme which worked, from 2007 till 2017 around was telecom. When the COVID Struck Indian market long sleeping Pharma and chemical companies jumped into a sudden Bull Run.

Base mindset

You don't need any specific market scenario to trade this strategy, as at every time some or other industry will be markets favourite, rather you need to be a very active trader to keep looking for sectorial opportunities available in the market. In recent times in early 2022 when Russia and Ukraine two of the fine size commodities producers of the world faced off, the commodity market fired all cylinders. Crude crossed $130 in a very short time. A lot of people captured early opportunity in technology stocks during COVID times. So, basically you need to keep looking at the market and industry factors and for sure you will find some of the gems sitting in a corner to be found and outperform.

Look for the place to enter

As we have already discussed earlier that finding the best industry is the most important task, once you have done it rest of the things remain easy, especially when you can read the charts. We can either buy them on a breakout to new 50-day highs or in anticipation of a breakout. In a rising market, most industry momentum will give a breakout someday. We can look for some pullbacks towards a rising 10, 20 or 50 day EMAs in stocks a certain uptrend.

Always keep in mind that winners will always be very silent in the beginning, they will start roaring when they have shown some good levels on charts, identifying those ones early is the best thing you can do to make the most of the situation.

The Stoploss- yes it's the most important part!

Just keep the stoploss of 3-4% from your buy price or look at the strategy which you use as discussed in the book.

Two types of industries Investors do not expect to perform well each year are

1. Those that were up the most over the past 1-3 years, because no one believes they can go any higher.
2. Those that were down the most in the past 1-3 years because people have long written them off.

You just need to expect the unexpected. You will find most of them in above two. Industry momentum could be short-term -based on sector rotation or long-term based on a secular change.

Look at the quantity and risk capital

More than 1% of capital should not be risked in this strategy

Exit at the right point

Trader's strategic focus must be on hot industries. Finding a stock with range contraction that belongs to a currently favoured industry is the thing to do. When you do it with good technical stands you can easily make even 50% in a short span of time. Same technical Strategy when adopted in a not so favoured industry the profits can be restricted to the tune of 8 to 10%

What is it all about!

Sector rotation is something that happens constantly. Once it starts happening, it will last for a long period of time- weeks or even months and the markets or rather market conditions will keep throwing opportunities towards the trader. One most important thing which market participants need to understand that we must do a mix of understanding both industry and stocks beneath it. Industries are a bit easy to identify as the market keeps sending various signals for the conformation but sometime the trader gets stuck into a wrong stock of a right industry.

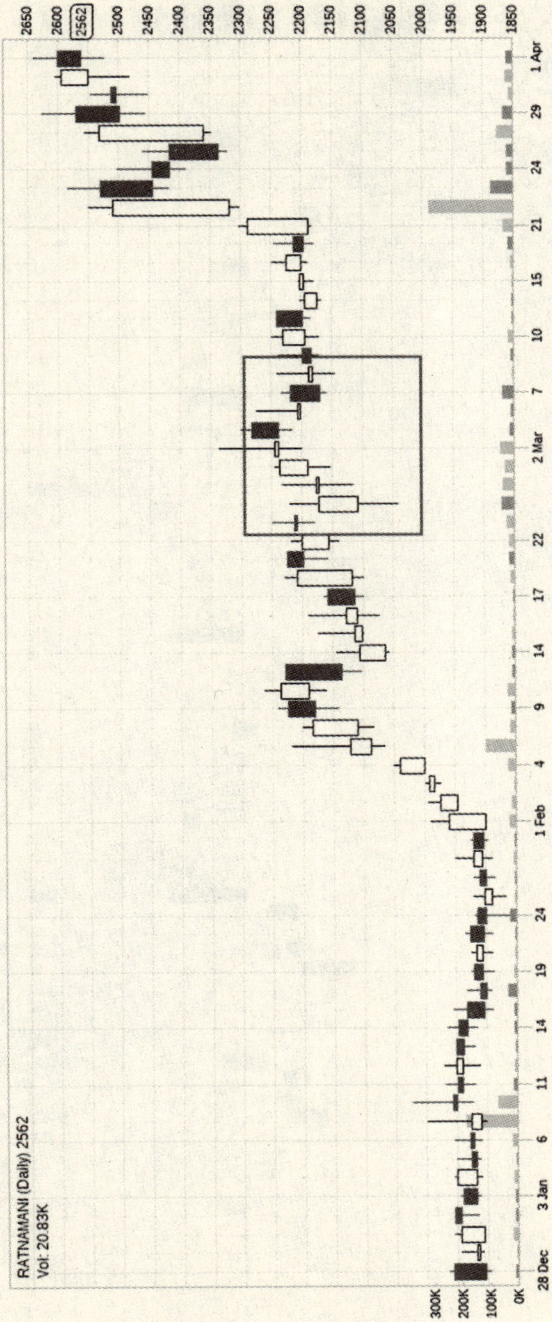
RATNAMANI (Daily) 2562
Vol: 20.83K

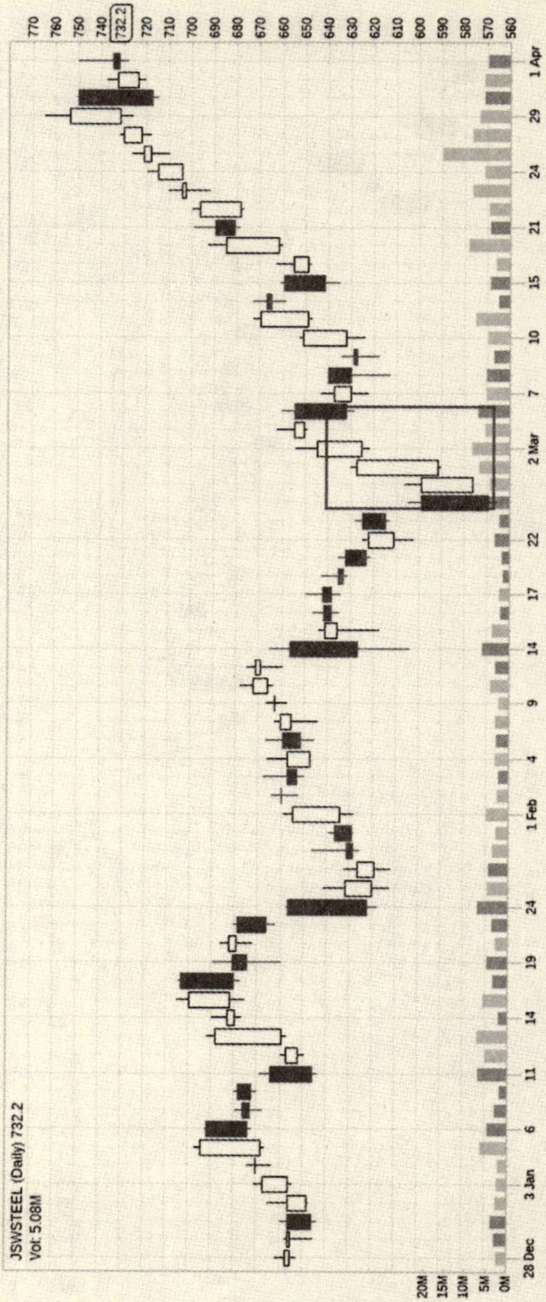
JSWSTEEL (Daily) 732.2
Vol: 5.08M

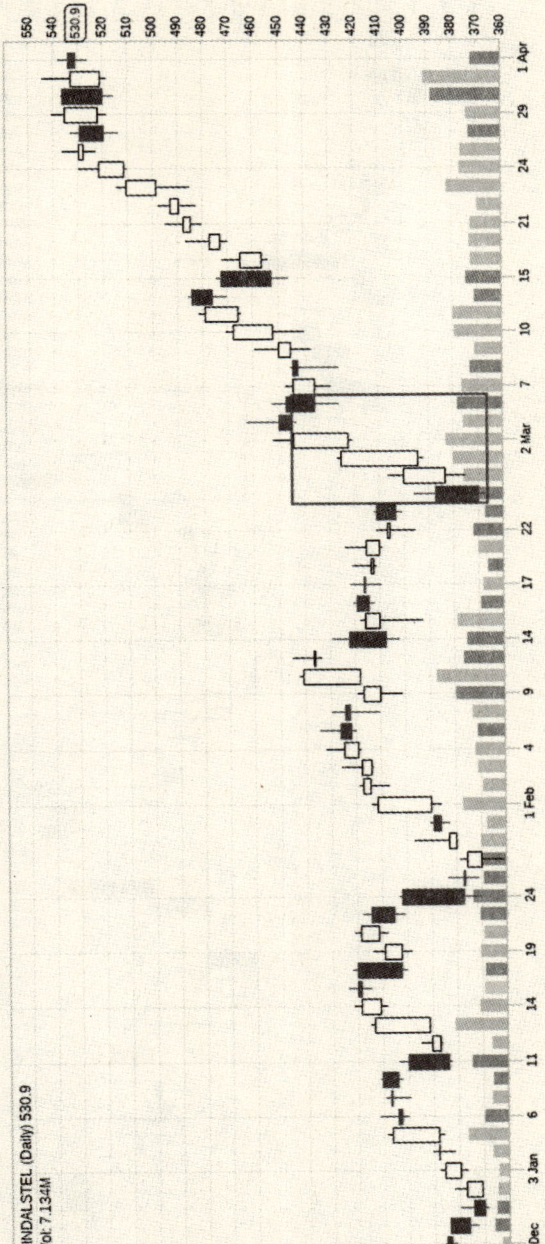
JINDALSTEL (Daily) 530.9
Vol: 7.134M

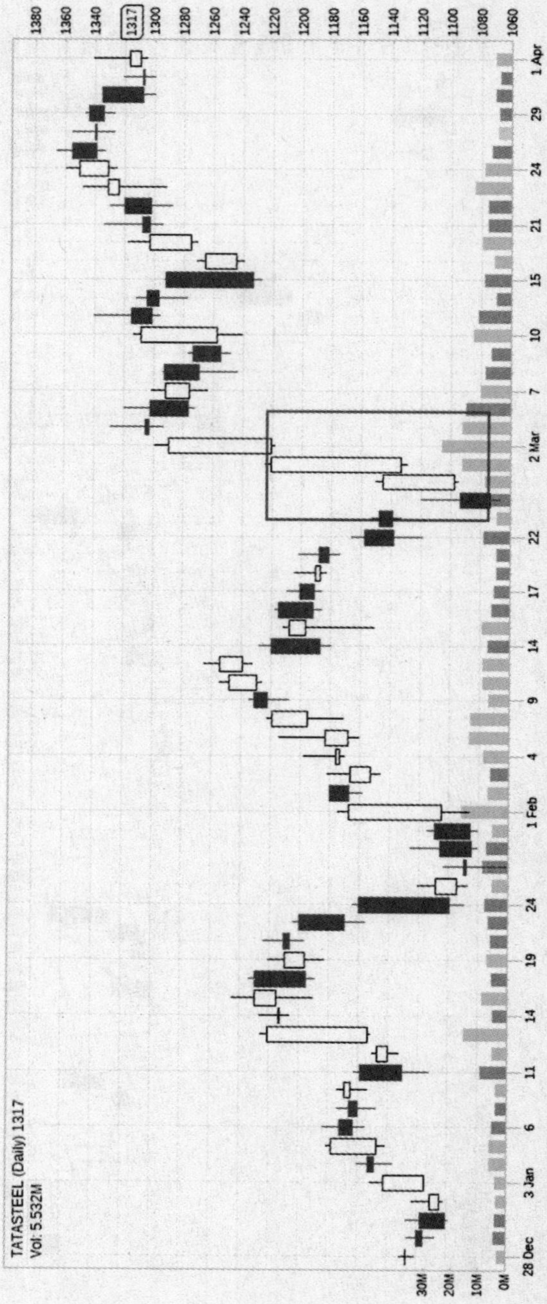
TATASTEEL (Daily) 1317
Vol: 5.532M
1380
1360
1340
1317
1300
1280
1260
1240
1220
1200
1180
1160
1140
1120
1100
1080
1060
30M
20M
10M
0M
28 Dec
3 Jan
6
11
14
19
24
1 Feb
4
9
14
17
22
2 Mar
7
10
15
21
24
29
1 Apr

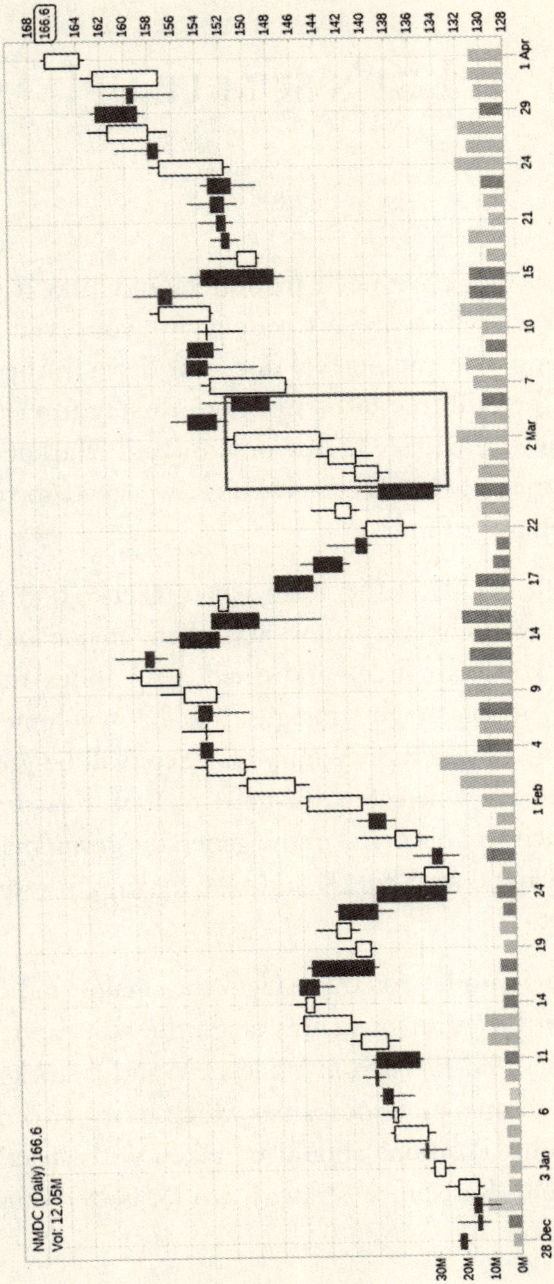
NMDC (Daily) 166.6
Vol: 12.05M
168
166.6
164
162
160
158
156
154
152
150
148
146
144
142
140
138
136
134
132
130
128
30M
20M
10M
0M
28 Dec
3 Jan
6
11
14
19
24
1 Feb
4
9
14
17
22
2 Mar
7
10
15
21
24
29
1 Apr

LET'S SUM IT UP!

At this stage we need to understand that it is the bull market which makes money for you even while you are sleeping. But the market does not drive in the same gear always. The bull market is not here to stay forever and that is why the strategies which works in Bull Market might not make money always. To tackle this, we need to understand various phases of market.

Bullish - This is the stage where every good stock keep hitting new high every now and then, major indices be it NIFTY, Mid Cap Index and Small Cap Index trades above 50 EMA, at this stage strategies like IPO, volume blast and breakout will make money for you. There will be green-shoots in market everywhere but we need to look for some greener places which will outperform the generally strong market. Keep your risk capital at .5 to 1% and take maximum returns out of the market.

Range-bound- At this stage the major indices trends to trade within a range, at this stage the risk capital must be reduced to .25% - .50% from 1% level. Wait for stocks' quarterly earnings and then pick companies which have performed better in the results. Positions should be taken with strict stop loss. Support and Resistance strategy works better during range bound market.

Bearish- In a confirmed downtrend all three major indices NIFTY, Mid Cap Index and Small Cap Index will be found below 50 EMA. At this stage of market, we must be sitting mostly on cash or short. Don't be too adventurous in market. Do not buy breakout as in down trend most of them will fail. It is probably selling time, be patient, stay in touch with market, keep close watch and get yourself ready for next new opportunity when it comes you must be ready with your learnings and time tested strategy.

Bottoming process- Bear market create fear in the mind of investors. When market turn up to begin the next up move loaded with opportunities most investors do not believe.

Bottom will happen when you and most of the participants will least expect, when all news will be negative, all of sudden market will take new personality, most investors will not believe in uptrend but all the practical strategies discussed in the book will start working for you. It's the stage when the fall is captured and the market is ready to make its next move. The next move may be a consolidation or a slight uptrend, may be bigger uptrend or may be relief rally or a dead cat bounce.

Put call ratio can help to confirm you that market is very near to bottom, may be ready for at least a dead cat bounce.

Following strategies can be very useful at this stage:

1. **Mean reversion at select stocks**- Once you see the market is bottoming out, get into trades in those stocks which are beaten down badly and wait for around 10 weeks. You can see gains in the range of 50 to 100%
2. **Relative strength**- while the markets were falling, keep your eye on those ones which were showing consolidation,

once the bottoming process is over these stock will create wonders.

A single strategy will never work in the markets, because the market behaviour is ever changing. The only thing which a trader has to do wisely is to keep tracking the trend and changing the strategy accordingly. So get prepared, study hard, do your homework, the historically tested Strategies discussed in the book will work for you. You just need to give some time to read and re-read the strategies. It will definitely consume few hours and days & demand study from your end, but it is a valuable skill which you can learn in your life.

Remember, you don't have to behave like a Bull or a Bear. You just have to behave like a trader and business man who is here to make money.

AT THE END.....

Stop loss is the most important- this is the beginning and this is the end, in any case never forget your stop losses. It is a sacrosanct level which you must follow always. Keeping a stop loss will protect your capital and keep you alive in the market to be relevant.

The main reason so many investors lose money in stock market is that they do not have a defense. They do not know how to protect themselves from losses. They do not know why they should always use stop loss. Buying a stock without knowing when to sell is just like driving a bike without knowing when and how to use brakes.

Don't be ashamed of making mistakes while you invest. Just own them, learn from them, and If price fall below a certain percentage of your actual price, accept your mistake that you went wrong and exit from that trade to move onto next. There will be hundreds of new opportunities in the market.

Never let yourself get discouraged by temporary setback. It is definitely possible to make more than 40% per annum once you develop the strategy that works for you in the stock market. By reading this book you can have proper foundation and strategies to be a successful swing trader.

Life and trading has no place for rigidity- We enter in market and we do it with some perception, having this perception is always good as we must do everything with a pre thought out condition. The problem is about being rigid. A trader keeps working on a single strategy doesn't want to change it even when the market is changing itself. Here let's take an example of COVID era in January February 2020, when the market started behaving in an extreme manner, Strong bullish pattern changed to extreme bearish. A lot of traders got stuck in false hopes and we all know what happened next. Market made its final bottom on 23 March 2020 far lower than anyone expected at 7511 Nifty.

On the day worst news of lock down came due to COVID, Market made its bottom and suddenly bearish pattern changed to bullish and market started moving up, leaving opportunity behind. Most of investors are still suffering with FOMO. (Fear of missing out)

Take a clean sweep, define your goals- Let me refer a book beyond this one which you all must read. The Greatness Guide by Robin S Sharma is an amazing collection of some short strategies for life. One of the chapters in the book is about "taking a clean sweep". The chapter says that sometime we must take a break from everything what we do. Take a holiday and cut off yourself from the daily activities. It's not necessary to trade every day. The market is going to remain here always. Taking a clean sweep will give you some space and time to reconsider your goals about what you want to achieve in life and trading.

300 strategy- Perseverance is what you need sometime. Watch a movie 300 where only 300 soldiers from Sparta fought till the end. What important is that they didn't fight with courage only, rather they had a strategy in place. The strategy is very important before you enter any field or activity. It will allow you to stay long in the market. Study the market before you enter in that. If you have a strong strategy for it you can make large money even with a small capital. The same way 300 soldiers destroyed a large army in front of them.

There is abundance of money to be lent, don't borrow from everywhere- In last so many years the economic growth has done one good thing to us. Money is available everywhere at a single click. Banks, NBFCs are flooded with money to be lent. It's good to borrow but it's very bad to be over leveraged. Even if you feel that in next one month any stock is going to get doubled then also don't get leveraged too much for it, it's the worst risk which a trader can take. If you want to take non-calculated risk go and play roulette in a casino where chance of winning is at least 50%. Keep your finances under control else the market will teach you by the harder way.

Travel through the market, destination is not your concern- Trading is a journey not the destination. Don't define targets about what you want to earn, keep following your good strategy, we may say strategy with an edge will let you make money always. Don't think about how much gains you will make. You can't set the targets; the markets can do it for you. Keep working and keep trading, market will keep rewarding your strategy and process.

At the end I would like to say…keep learning new ways to trade in markets, it's full of wonders and ways to make money. Success need opportunity and the stock market and Dalal Street gives everyone a lot of opportunities every year. Just focus on how good student you are. Work on your weakness until it becomes your strength. In this process you need to unlearn many things you follow, many thoughts you have about the market which are not working. Just start learning new time tested strategies which have an edge in the market.

There is just one difference in the successful and not so successful investors and traders is that the successful ones keep learning and do the things which others are not doing.

Persistence is the key when learning to invest, if you are still with me you are ready to follow a set of buying and selling rules. Your objective is not to buy at the bottom but to buy when your probability of being right is highest. You will follow your strategy and during this process you will take stop loss as tuition fee to Dalal Street.

All the best and happy investing….